The 15 Minute Formula

How Busy Moms Can Ditch the Guilt, Say Yes to What Matters, and Conquer Their Goals

Cara Harvey

For more information, email help@apurposedrivenmom.com

ISBN: 979-8-9853006-0-4

GET YOUR FREE GIFT!

To get the best experience with this book, I've found readers who download and use the 30-Day Action Guide are able to implement faster and take the next steps needed to manage your time and your goals!

You can get a copy by visiting:

www.the15minuteformula.com/free

To my heart and support system. To my family Ron, Dean, Arianna, and Isaiah. Thank you for supporting me through the long hours and time in the office so Mommy can reach her dreams and help other moms!

Table of Contents

Introduction

I remember the exact moment I became resentful of my family.

I was home with my newborn baby and my husband had gone back to work. It was me and her—alone for the first time since she was born.

I had left my teaching job to attempt to work full time in network marketing a few years prior. I had dreams of starting my own business and coaching company. I wanted more time freedom and the ability to make my own hours around my family and what actually mattered to us.

And here I was, lying on the floor of our playroom with my two-month-old, sobbing my eyes out.

I was covered in spit up (most likely from the day before), couldn't remember the last time I showered, and that fuzz on my teeth reminded me that I hadn't brushed them yet today. Surviving on a few hours of sleep, I watched my husband leave to go to work and thought, *What about me?*

How was I supposed to take care of my kids (my stepson at this point was nine years old) when my husband was at work? When was I supposed to have time to get back to work? What about those mounds of laundry eyeing me up from the corner? Would I ever have time to start the business I dreamed of having? Heck, I didn't even know when I'd be able to shower without the baby crying and me panicking.

Is this what motherhood was supposed to be like?

Over the course of those first few months with my husband back at work, my resentfulness toward him started to grow. I mean, he got to leave the house and have real conversations each day with coworkers. He was able to work at a job he loved and have a purpose outside of parenthood. He didn't feel the pressure of having to take care of the home, the kids, and everything in between.

On top of these feelings, during this time of my life, I was dealing with Postpartum Anxiety and Depression (PPA/PPD) that my doctors dismissed as "baby blues." I spent months suffering in silence because I thought I was just an unfit mother. I mean, what kind of mother struggles to feel fulfilled at home?

Shouldn't "just being Mom" be enough?

I started to take these feelings out on my family. Due to my PPA/PPD, I struggled to know how to handle my own feelings and emotions and, since the doctor said I would "get over it," I thought there was something wrong with me for feeling unfulfilled, anxious, and angry.

Instead of "just getting over it," I buried my feelings down. I was afraid to talk about them because of what others would think. And instead of dealing with these feelings, I dove into wearing busy like a badge of honor.

I thought if I just kept going, if I checked everything off my to-do list, if I appeared to be working harder than everyone else, then I was doing a good job.

I mean that is what a mom does, right? Martyr themselves for their family? Grind themselves down to serve? Put everyone else's needs first?

Along the way, I had forgotten about my needs.

Over the course of the next few years, I did what I knew how to do. I hustled. I worked hard. I did my best as a mom, worked my network marketing business during nap time, and stayed up late trying to do it all.

And people would affirm my grind.

"Wow—you do so much! I wish I could be like you!"

"I seriously don't know how you do it all, it's amazing!"

"I wish I could do what you do."

Because on the outside, it looked amazing. I was running my home and family (and at this point was pregnant with kid number three). I was leading a successful network marketing business with 200+ people on my team. I was posting motivational quotes on social media like I was a Pinterest page. And I did it all with a smile on my face. I *loved* that people thought I was successful. I loved that they thought I had it all together.

I had tied my worth to accomplishing my day-to-day tasks, and a completed to-do list meant that I was beating my mental health issues and anxiety. In my eyes, that completed to-do list meant I "had it together" more than other moms. That finished list told me each day whether I was worthy or not.

But on the inside, I was drowning.

I wasn't resting. I equated burnout with success. I was burnt out, overwhelmed, and irritated all the time. And when I wasn't accomplishing things, I thought there was something wrong with me. I thought I was a failure. I thought that I'd never have it all together like that mom I saw on Instagram with the beautiful kitchen, well-dressed kids, and curated perfection on their social media feed.

In addition to the major burnout, while I was pregnant with kid three, our outwardly perfect-looking family went through a major upheaval. My husband, our primary breadwinner, lost his job and was unemployed for eight months. We were on government assistance, almost filed bankruptcy, and I was selling anything I could on Facebook Marketplace to get by.

After my son was born, I once again was struggling with PPA/PPD, and this time, I became an advocate for myself. I went to multiple doctors. I got into therapy. I realized that hustling and not resting was actually making things worse.

I realized it was time to change the way I was living so I could ditch the burnout. I needed to make changes that allowed me to stop going a million miles an hour and carve out time for myself. I knew that hustling the way I was would lead to resentful feelings toward my family when they weren't moving at my pace. And I was moving farther away from the mother I wanted to be.

That's when I developed this system of the 15 Minute Formula that I am going to share with you in this book.

Once I started to use these principles in my life, things began to shift. I started to feel more joy in my home. I was spending more time playing with my kids. I lost the guilt that came from a sink full of dishes or piles of laundry begging to be folded.

I crafted time pockets for me: to read, to watch TV, to call family, or to just *be*. And I finally took the leap into growing my own business where I could help overwhelmed moms find time for their goals too—without the overwhelm or burnout.

Because I know what it's like.

I know how it can be to feel like you're sinking. I know what it feels like to get lost in motherhood. I know what it's like to feel angry that you don't have time to pee alone—let alone pursue your goals.

In this book, I'm going to walk you through the 5 Pillars to help you go from overwhelmed to in control.

These pillars include

- Vision
- Time management and productivity
- Goal setting
- Routines
- Habits

But before you dive in, I want to give you some encouragement. Because this book is going to be different from a lot of other productivity books out there.

Because we are moms.

And our lives are different. We *need* a different system.

The 15 Minute Formula is not about perfection, it's about intention.

We'll be diving into what I call "priority-based productivity"—because it's not about just doing more. **It's about fitting in time for more of what matters to you and your family.**

There is no one-size-fits-all here. I want you to take what I teach and customize it for what you need at the moment.

The 15 Minute Formula isn't about jamming a million things into your already overflowing to-do list or being the perfect mom. It's about making life work for you *while* working on your goals—without adding a million things to your plate.

In this book, I'll also be sharing stories of other moms from all different backgrounds. These moms have applied the principles I teach and have been able to customize them to find massive happiness in their lives. From stay-at-home moms to single moms to moms working the night shift and more—I hope you'll be able to see yourself in their stories.

And because I want this book to do more than sit on your shelf (no judgment, I have plenty of pretty books collecting dust too), at the end of each chapter will be short action items that will help you apply that pillar.

If you haven't already, make sure you go to www. the15minuteformula.com/free to download the 30-day Action Guide. This guide will break down your reading of the book *and* the actions to help you read and implement all that we'll be chatting about.

I want this book to feel like you and me are hanging out at the Target café, talking about managing #allthethings while our kids eat cake pops and ask to play in the toy aisle a million times.

So, if you're ready to stop spinning your wheels, done feeling like you're never doing enough, and tired of being tied to your to-do list, let's do this!

Introduction Action Steps

1. Download the 30-Day Action Guide at www. the15minuteformula.com/free to help you read and implement these tips in the next thirty days.

2. Grab a notebook to take notes in—this way you can always go back to it. If you want to go digital, I've also linked a Trello board with the book chapters (you'll hear me mention Trello a few times in this book, it's an amazing tool!) where you can keep all your notes, thoughts, and ideas. You'll get this when you snag your action guide!

3. And if you're ready, I want you to email me at book@ apurposedrivenmom.com with the subject line "I'm over the overwhelm." In the email, it's time to draw a line in the sand. Send me two sentences (or more if you want) saying, "I am committing to me! I am over being a burnout mom, and I deserve this!" This commitment is your first lesson in public accountability. If you want more, take a picture of that email and the book cover and tag me on Instagram at @apurposedrivenmom. Share with your people that you're ready to remember how fabulous *you* are again!

PILLAR #1

CREATING YOUR PRIORITY-BASED VISION

Chapter 1

Crafting Your Own Vision

We're going to dive into the 5 Pillars of the 15 Minute Formula, but before we begin, I want to remind you of something.

There is no cookie-cutter printable that will actually help you achieve your goals.

You need to be willing to customize. You need to be willing to say no to some things and yes to others. You need to be willing to be messy. You need to be ready to ditch perfection for a life that you're actually excited to live.

So, are we on the same page?

Cool.

Let's dive in.

You've gotten lost on the social media scroll, right?

You open Instagram to check your notifications real quickly before folding your laundry, and all of a sudden, it's one hour later and all you've done is scroll through image after image of moms that seem to "have it all together." Now you feel even less motivated to do what you have to get done, and you feel like you're the worst, ugliest, most hot mess (Insert your negative self-talk of choice here.) mom in the world and want to crawl under the blankets and never come out again.

A wise friend of mine Krystle once told me that if you find yourself scrolling someone's page for more than five minutes, you're either judging them or comparing yourself to them.

Ouch.

It wasn't until then that I truly saw how harmful implanting someone else's vision of a perfect life was and the negative impact it was having on me.

Even though things were going great—I had a thriving business, a happy marriage, kids that didn't drive me crazy every single minute of the day (well most days)—I still felt not good enough. It still felt like something was missing in my life.

I realized that the missing piece was coming from comparison, it was coming from other people's curated highlight reels, and it was coming from not having a vision of what I truly wanted my life to be like.

Throughout this book, you're going to hear me talk a lot about "priority-based productivity" because that is truly what I believe the missing piece is for so many of us— PRIORITY being the keyword here.

The methods you are going to continue to read about in this book are *all* about being proactive. I'll be sharing some reactive strategies too because heck, we need that as well. But starting right now, I want to encourage you to become proactive about your life. It's time to stop letting life happen to us and become active participants.

Before we jump into creating priorities (and trust me, we'll be flipping this word on its head in the next chapter), I want us to start with the end in mind.

We're going to start with creating a vision.

Now, this vision is more than a vision board that you make on January 1. Don't get me wrong, I love vision boards, but I think if we're going to create a priority-based life for you, we need to get specific about what *you* want this season of your life to be like.

Embracing the Seasons of Your Life

When I was struggling with resentment toward my husband and my family, it was because I was looking at others. I was looking at how my life used to be, and I wasn't embracing the season of motherhood I was in.

Because it's hard.

Each season of your life and motherhood has so much beauty in it—but let's be honest, sometimes it feels like a dumpster fire.

And if you don't truly look at your season and make a realistic plan, you'll be setting yourself up to fail.

We have this notion as moms that we have to "do it all." We struggle with trying to get it all done so that we look the busiest and most successful and like we're killing this mom game. (Hand raised over here too.)

What if instead of feeling like we have to "do it all" right now, we pause, slow down, and determine what is the most important in this season.

You can look at seasons in a few ways. Literally using the seasons on the calendar or chunking your life and months into their own seasons.

While I am going to encourage you to do a lot of quarterly planning and time-based thinking in this book, can we get one thing out of the way first?

You don't need to be married to the calendar.

Stop letting the first of the month dictate that you need to have it all together or the last of the month to be a closing out of things. You don't have to wait until Monday to start.

You can determine your season, you can determine your start date, and you're in charge of whatever end date you want to use.

Okay—while that's out of the way, let's start to create a vision for your season.

I want you to think about the next twelve months of your life. Use the chart below as a guide for this or make sure to go to www.the15minuteformula.com/free to grab the 30-Day Action Guide for this book.

Looking at the next few months, jot down the events you may have going on, the times when you know a hefty work project is coming up, and even when you're going on vacation. I want you to step back and think about the future and look at what you have happening in the near future.

month	event
JANUARY	Nothing Really!
FEBRUARY	Lots of Family Birthdays
MARCH	Family Vacation
APRIL	Big Yearly Work Event
MAY	Nothing Really!
JUNE	End of School
JULY	Kids Home for Summer
AUGUST	Family Vacation
SEPTEMBER	Back to School
OCTOBER	Fall Sports Start
NOVEMBER	Holidays
DECEMBER	Holidays

It's key before you start any project, tackle any goal, or create any routines in your home that you start with the end in mind—and that begins with creating seasons.

Based on what you have coming up, I want you to identify a few seasons for yourself—write these right next to the events you notice you have coming up. These seasons can be a month-long or three months long or even six months long—that is up to you (yes, I'm asking you to trust yourself enough to determine this. You can do it!). I find that by making sure I have these seasons mapped out, I am less likely to burn out because I'm not in hustle mode all the time.

Four seasons to include:

- A season of rest and fun
- A season of productivity
- A season of busy
- A season of planning

Now, this isn't to say in your season of rest you won't work on any goals, but perhaps, that is a season where you take things lighter and don't put as many commitments on your plate. This also doesn't mean that during your season of productivity you're hustling and staying up all hours of the night to get things done and never resting—this is just the focus for this season.

When you start with the end in mind and really look at where you want to go, you can intentionally plan periods for everything you want to get done.

You may have heard the phrase, "Women can have it all, but not at the same time," which I originally heard from Madeline Albright. And it's true.

Instead of always shoving your schedules full until they explode with tasks and goals, why don't you instead create a focused plan for that time period that makes sense?

Here's an example of how I might determine my seasons for the next few months.

Let's work backwards.

I know that August, September, and October get super busy in our home. My oldest plays travel basketball, which includes a lot of driving. My five-year-old just started kindergarten, and we've signed her up for cheerleading and Girl Scouts, and my four-year-old is playing flag football for the first time.

My husband is an administrator of a school, so the back-to-school season is super hectic for him, and often, this is a time where I know I need to do a lot more around the house than normal since he's away.

Here are my options:

1. Keep our schedule hectic and also say yes to other church activities that get brought up. Add a big work project on my plate too and then feel irritated because my husband isn't home as much and I have to "do it all." Spend most of my days mumbling under my breath about how "Mom has to always do everything," stress out, and hit up the drive-through most nights—

which makes us go over our budget and causes me to stress eat, and then blow up and yell at the slightest irritation because I'm burnt out.

2. Realize this is a busy season and plan ahead for it. I could use June and July to create a three-month meal plan and bag up freezer meals to make evenings easier. I could also declutter in the summer, so it makes picking up the house quicker and less of a mess. I could have a conversation with my husband about back to school and where I really need support and ask him how I could best support him. Since I've done this activity for the entire year, I know that February and March are busy seasons for me with work since I host the annual Purpose Driven Mom Summit, and I'll need the same help he needs now during those months.

By pausing and taking a step back to look at the next few months, I can create a vision based on my seasons instead of just jamming it all in and feeling like I'm sloppily surviving. Knowing when my busy season is allows me to also make sure I intentionally schedule in a season of rest and a season of planning. This also helps me ditch the guilt when I am working extra hours because I know that I'll have more time for family activities later on.

One student of mine, Arwen F., used this same process when the pandemic hit. Arwen is a stay-at-home mom of four kids who are 23, 20, 18, and 13. Arwen has a dream of starting her own business helping moms gamify the cleaning experience and get their houses in order (something I know I need desperately!).

We had worked together in coaching sessions to pick the dates her course would launch, and she was plugging along and on track until the pandemic hit in 2020. Instead of the time she thought she'd have to get it all done, she now had to trek across multiple states to pick up her kids from college and figure out new school-at-home schedules. Her house was loud with the noise of kids, and the main goal was to keep everyone on task and fed.

And while Arwen wanted to keep on the schedule we created for her course launch, she knew that if she tried to continue to pile it on in an already hectic season, it wouldn't get done well and she'd be exhausted.

So, she decided to pause the course a bit to focus on her current season and family for that moment. She decided to launch the course a few months later when life would have adjusted a bit and she could put in the time the course deserved.

Fast forward a few months and, while everyone was still home and her house felt a bit chaotic, she was able to space out the work, finish her first course, and launch her business into the world.

She didn't let the guilt of moving her timeline make her feel like a failure. She didn't completely dismiss her goal forever but instead pushed it to a time that made more sense.

Because that's the best part about recognizing and embracing your seasons—you don't have to put things off forever, burn yourself out just because you must do it all at once, and you can ditch the guilt of not hustling all the time.

Anchoring Into a Word of the Season

Since we're talking about seasonality and vision, I want to touch on something that I've added into my goal setting that has helped keep me anchored and that's the Word of the Year.

I originally read about this concept in the book *The One Word That Will Change Your Life* by Jon Gordon. This is how he describes using "One Word" in your life.

"One Word that will change your life is a proven way to create clarity, power, passion, and life change. Each year resolutions are rarely kept, and goals are often easily forgotten, but One Word sticks. By living a single word that is meant for you, you'll find renewed purpose and meaning throughout the year and laser-like focus and power for your life."[1]

While I loved the concept of picking a word for the entire year, I learned that it was really tricky to want to stick with one word since my days, weeks, and months were ever changing.

Once I embraced using seasonality in my goal setting and productivity, I realized that instead of doing a word of the year, I could customize it and pick a word of the quarter, word of the season, or even word of the month.

I've mentioned before that you can take all we talk about and make it work for you, and that's exactly what I did with this concept. At first, it felt like I was cheating—I mean, shouldn't I be able to stick with one word all year?

But then I realized that thinking it was cheating was an ingrained mindset. It was a lesson I had somehow learned along the way that was making me struggle to actually implement the concept.

And in this case, the lesson was that if I didn't follow something to a T, then I was doing it wrong. I learned this lesson as a kid who wanted to believe that if I got on the honor roll, I was better than my sisters. I also learned it when I would get accolades as a teacher for always completing my IEP (Individualized Education Plans) for my students with the most detail and without much correction needed.

Along the way, I had gotten it stuck in my mind that in order to be "successful," I needed to do everything perfectly.

And as I started to create the 15 Minute Formula and really dive into priority-based productivity, I realized the *power* of customization. It became so freeing for me to recognize that things don't always have to be perfect, they don't always have to follow all the "rules," and I can make them fit into my life.

As a busy mom of three, I started to see that the productivity and time management tips that worked for a single male working at a Fortune 500 company (which is who most productivity books are geared toward) weren't going to work for me. It was time to realize the control of having to fit my productivity in a box and decide how I wanted to do it.

Hence, creating a word for *whatever* you need.

When you're thinking of your word of the season, I want to encourage you to think about how you want to feel at the end of that time period. The goal of creating a word is to make a vision for yourself, to craft a plan that helps you get there and that allows you to theme your focus and your priorities.

I typically encourage moms to create a word for each quarter because it's easier to stick with a word for a few months before deciding whether to keep or change your word. If you're struggling to think about a vision for that long in the future or it seems overwhelming, just start with a word of the month.

Brainstorm adjectives that describe the feelings you want to have at the end. Do you want to be more confident? Have more fun? Be more creative? Embrace intention? The sky really is the limit!

Some of my favorite past words have been aligned, intention, and impact (which is my current word at the time of me writing this book).

Once you've got it down to about five words, pick the one that makes the most sense for you during this season. Can you see how we're always looping back up to your season? Because it wouldn't make sense for your word of the quarter to be relax if you have a heavy work season. Or it wouldn't fit to make your word driven if you've already decided to slow down for the holidays.

word of the season

FOCUS	IMPROVE	PASSION	STILLNESS
GROW	STRENGTH	JOY	SERENITY
ORGANIZE	ENCOURAGE	NOW	VISION
SIMPLIFY	WAKE	UNLIMITED	WISDOM
BLOOM	PRESENT	KINDNESS	VULNERABILITY
BRAVE	BEAUTY	PLAY	ADVENTURE
INSPIRE	ENTHUSIASM	THOUGHTFUL	EXAMPLE
THRIVE	CONNECT	DELIBERATE	COMFORT
GRADITUDE	ALIGNMENT	TRUST	GIVE
CONSISTENCY	PRIORITY	CONSCIOUS	RISE
BALANCE	CREATE	INCREASE	BARE
BE	NEW	BREATHE	PERSPECTIVE
WORTH	FAITH	COMMIT	GLOW
ELEVATE	BELIEVE	SEEK	FORGIVE
TODAY	TRANSFORM	PAUSE	OBSERVE
LESS	INTEGRITY	FORWARD	SOUL
MINDFUL	GENTLE	CHANGE	DELIGHT
CONSIDERATE	EXPANSION	LISTEN	PATIENCE
CALM	GROUNDED	FREE	CULTIVATE
POSITIVITY	HARMONY	BUILD	SMILE
RESPECT	ACTION	FLOURISH	MEDITATE
APPRECIATE	AMBITION	MOVE	LEAD
ENLIGHTEN	PURPOSE	RENEW	CELEBRATE
INTENTIONAL	HERE	PROGRESS	MORE
FLOW	DREAM	EXPLORE	REFLECT
FAMILY	MAGIC	FINISH	LIGHT
SLOW	SHINE	RELAX	HEART
POSSIBILITY	DETERMINATION	PRAY	ALWAYS
PERSEVERE	PEACE	SPARKLE	COMPASSION
LOVE	TRY	REPRESENT	ENERGY
HOPE	TEACH	WHOLE	SACRED
FEARLESS	COMPROMISE	JOURNEY	PERSIST
HAPPY	IMAGINE	PROSPER	BRIDGE
SPIRIT	LEARN	CONTRIBUTE	COURAGE
GLORIOUS	WONDER	DISCIPLINE	ENOUGH
GRACE	EMBRACE	LAUGH	STRIVE
TRUTH	HUMBLE	HERE	WISH
BELONG	WORK	SHIFT	MOMENTUM

What to Do Once You've Picked Your Word of the Season

Now that you've got your word, you'll want to create a plan around it and create a vision of what it will actually look like in your life. This vision is something we'll anchor back into during each chapter and phase of the 15 Minute Formula.

You'll want to make your word visible because if something isn't visible, you'll forget about it. Make it your lock screen, write it on your planner, or stick it on Post-it Notes around your house.

The goal of this is to remind yourself of the person you said you wanted to be at the end of the quarter (or your determined time period). Whenever you make decisions like "Should I say yes or no to this?" or "Does this action align with who I want to be?" run your word through it.

Will this bring me more *joy?*

Does this give me more *consistency?*

Will this action allow me to be *happier?*

Apply it to whatever your word is.

If the answer is no, then this might be a goal, task, or activity you put off until it makes more sense. Again, priority-based productivity isn't about saying no to everything or never going after what matters. It's about determining what makes sense for you, your family, and your goals in this current season.

But we're not going to stop there.

I want you to really dream and create this vision for yourself.

Take a piece of paper and split it into the main categories of your life. This could be family, work, spirituality, budgeting, etc., . . . I want you to ask yourself this question for each category.

"What would it look like if I showed up (insert your word here) for my (insert category here)?"

So, an example for me could be "What would it look like if I showed up to make an impact in my relationships?"

Underneath that, I could list things like send a daily text to a friend, Venmo $5 to someone to treat themself to coffee each week, call a family member once a week, or have a monthly Zoom with friends who I can't see in person.

Really start to dream about how the you in the future would show up for your word in those areas. Once a week, refer back to your chart. Ask yourself if you did show up this way and, if not, how you could keep going.

I'll be honest, I've had things on my list that I said I was going to do that never actually happened. But, because I was checking in with them weekly, they stayed top of mind, and I kept trying my best to show up that way.

Some Other Ways to Use Your Word of the Season

There are a lot of other ways you can make your word fluid and something that you actually use. Check out the list below for examples you can add in.

If you need more help with picking a word of the year, make sure to head to www.the15minuteformula.com/free so you can get the 15 Minute Formula Action Guide and a list of 100 words that you can pick from!

Examples of ways to use your word:

- Pick a book for that area
- Create affirmations for your word
- Find podcasts that help support your word
- Take a course around your word
- Journal daily about how you showed up for your word

Chapter 1 Action Steps

1. Map out your seasons over the course of the next year to start to create your vision.
2. Determine your word for each season and create your chart of what that will look and feel like.
3. Find one book, podcast, or course you can add to help you grow in that area.

Chapter 2

How to Actually Prioritize

"Just pick your priorities."

"You're just not prioritizing well."

"If it was really important to you, you'd prioritize time for it."

"We all have the same twenty-four hours."

Maybe you've heard some iteration of those phrases in your life.

I mean *clearly* your problem with productivity is a priority one, right?

Maybe not.

For a long time, I believed all of these statements. I thought that if I wasn't being productive or achieving my goals, it was my fault because I didn't prioritize well.

And over the past few years, I've realized the problem with the way that we've been taught to look at our priorities.

Now, don't get me wrong—you need to prioritize. Your goals and routines are not just going to magically happen if you don't create time for them.

When we don't create priorities, we get stuck in overwhelm. Everything feels important and urgent, and often, we're left with more things falling off our plan than getting crossed off our list.

Let's think about how we can strategically prioritize as moms.

Because if I were to ask a mom her top priority, I know she's going to say her kids—which makes complete sense.

So, how do we create time for all of the goals we want to work on when we're just focusing on one priority at a time? When our kids' needs always take precedence, where do we fit time in for us?

Let's stop just saying "I need to just prioritize things" and instead start to look at micro priorities.

Micro Priorities

A game changer for me when it came to managing my day was when I started to look at my micro priorities instead of lumping everything in together. When you look at these micro priorities, you can not only create time for multiple things that matter but also use the vision you've already created to pick and choose what exactly makes sense in this season.

What is a micro priority?

When we look at priorities, we essentially mean what is the most important *at this moment.*

The "at this moment" is KEY.

Last chapter, we spent time talking about seasonality and how important it is, and I want you to take that mindset into this chapter.

To determine your micro priorities, I want you to create a list of all the main areas of roles or categories in your life.

These could include

- Mom
- Wife
- Sister
- Daughter
- Work
- Hobbies
- Health
- Spirituality
- And more

See how I've mixed up roles and categories in this example. I want you to come up with six to nine of the areas that are most important to you in your current season or for the next twelve weeks.

Once you have your categories, write down two to three tasks, goals, or habits you'd like to work on for the next quarter for each category. When you're done, you'll have a decent list of about fifteen items. (And don't forget to head to www.the15minuteformula.com/free to grab your action guide where I'll have this worksheet ready to go for you.)

Can we take a "Zach Morris Time Out"? Did you watch *Saved by the Bell* as a kid too? I always loved when Zach would pause and talk to the audience. Let's pretend that is what you and I are going to do right now.

I know this list of 15+ items might look and feel overwhelming right now. I need you and me to have some trust. Trust me that we'll get this list to a place where it doesn't feel scary and like you want to rip it up, throw this book to the side, and keep going.

Okay, time in!

For example, my list might look like this:

ROLE: MOM

Spend 15 minutes 1:1 with each kid daily.

Have a date night per kid each month.

Start family devotions at dinner.

CATEGORY: WORK

Finish the manuscript of the book (and yes, my goal was to finish it in twelve weeks).

Hire coaches for the Purpose Driven Mom Club.

Record four episodes for the podcast. (PS If you're a podcast listener, make sure you go search The Purpose

Driven Mom Show wherever you podcast so we can hang out!)

I would continue this until I have a list for each category and role that I want to focus on.

Once you've got your list, we need to go ahead and create your micro priorities.

Looking at your list, I want you to rank the tasks inside each role/category in order of importance. If you could *only* get one of these things accomplished in your twelve weeks, which would it be? You can't have any ties—you need to make a decision!

By doing this, you're not completely putting these goals off or saying you're not going to work on them this quarter; instead, you're creating a hierarchy of importance to help you make a vision for the quarter to stick to.

When we create too many goals to work on and try to prioritize everything at the same time, nothing really gets done and we leave ourselves feeling super overwhelmed. On the flip side, when we don't prioritize at all, we never make any progress on our goals (inside and outside of motherhood) and live a bit in survival mode.

In later chapters, I'm going to show you how to use the 15 Minute Formula to break your goals down and create an action plan for each week, but you need to start here first—with determining those micro priorities.

Before your quarter, month, or year begins, you need to make that seasonal vision and determine what truly are the top priorities in each area of your life—not just your life as a whole.

Now, as you go into each week, you can ask yourself, "What is the priority for *this area* of my life this week?" and work on the top things in multiple categories.

By having this vision for the quarter, you're constantly moving toward goals without putting a ton of pressure on you to "do it all right now." You just continue to move down each list as needed.

One of my clients Kellie T. followed this exact same process when trying to balance working from home, homeschooling, and being a mom. Kellie is a mom to a 2, 4, and 8-year-old and was trying to figure out how to coordinate everything on her plate. On top of her regular mom, work, and homeschooling duties, she also had a dream of starting a blog and a business.

To figure out how to get done what mattered to her, she went through this activity and created her micro priorities for each of the areas of her life.

She wanted to jump in and start her blog but realized that in this season, it would be putting way too much on her plate. When she went through and wrote down her priorities for the blog category, instead of shoving a million things in, she picked "get organized." So, while she was working on micro priorities in the other categories of her life, she spent the twelve weeks figuring out exactly what she had to do to even start the blog.

In doing this, she eliminated the pressure to just jump in and get it done now—which would have most likely stressed her out and thrown her other micro priorities off balance. She listened to podcasts, took courses, and watched videos to make a list of all the tasks needed to achieve her goal. She created a season of learning, where creating her plan was the micro priority instead of putting a million things on her plate right now.

This plan wasn't about her putting her goals off or not knowing how to prioritize starting the blog. The plan was about determining, based on all her other micro priorities for the season, what actually made sense right now.

When I asked Kellie how she felt about moving some pieces of her goal around to re-prioritize what fit into her season, she told me, " I'm more relaxed now and happier, you know? Like I can breathe. I have all this stuff I want to do. My four-year-old will be in kindergarten soon, and then in two years, all my kids will be in school, and the priority will change. And I'm okay with being able to still work on things with my blog, just at a slower pace than I planned."

Why It's More Than Your Why

We've already covered how the world has taught us to prioritize wrong, and now I want to pause to talk about another productivity misnomer out there.

Have you ever heard the phrase "Your why needs to be bigger than your excuses"?

I cannot *stand* this phrase.

And I used to shout it from the rooftops.

I was a school teacher for eight years, and when I left, I started to make money in network marketing. During that time, I got sucked into the hustle culture. I thought that if I didn't end the day at "inbox zero" and answer every message as soon as it came in, I was failing. I thought the reason I wasn't "successful" (and I say "successful" in quotes here) was because I didn't want it bad enough. In my three years as a full-time network marketer, I had grown a six-figure business and a team of 250 people. But because I didn't have a certain rank, which is one of the ways network marketing companies give out rewards and structure their pay, I thought I was failing.

And I spouted that trash from the rooftops. I wore hustle like a badge of honor and shamed others who didn't work as hard as me via social media posts and supposed motivational quotes.

I realized now how damaging that was to others and myself.

That phrase "your why isn't big enough" is rooted in shame and simply makes us feel like there is something wrong with us if we aren't successful.

Because, just like if I asked a mom about her priorities, she would mention her kids, she'd probably say the same thing about her why.

So, if we really break this down, telling a mom she doesn't want it or care about her why enough is essentially saying her kids aren't that important to her.

Let's quiet that noise.

There is nothing wrong with you, your motivation, your priorities, or your willpower if you're struggling to achieve a goal. It doesn't mean you don't care or your why isn't strong enough. It just means we need to make some tweaks to your plan.

Now don't get me wrong, I think you need something to motivate you. I love coming up with mission statements and vision boards and really knowing the *why* behind something.

But when we just continue to rely on motivation and our why to make us successful and productive, we're setting ourselves up for failure.

Because there will be days when we aren't motivated. Days where we just don't want to do it. Days where our kids are sick and we're exhausted and decluttering the hall closet or taking a class on learning the guitar is last on our list.

And that's okay.

Let's stop blaming ourselves and our willpower and instead, create a vision and a plan that lets us get things done when we're not feeling motivated *while* giving us the grace to make personalized decisions about our productivity.

Without making us feel lazy. Without making us feel shame. Without making us feel like we don't have it together like that mom we see on Instagram who has time to garden and make homemade snacks and go to the gym every day.

Let's make a plan—a plan that fits into your life and allows for you to make mistakes, get off track, and be a human being. Not one that shames you into feeling unworthy or like a failure.

And we're going to do this fifteen minutes at a time.

Chapter 2 Action Steps

1. Create Your micro priority chart for the next twelve weeks. Make sure you rank them so you know what needs to happen and in what order.

Chapter 3

Stop Relying on Your Motivation

As we begin to wind down this first section of the formula and move from vision to action, there is something I need to make sure you realize.

Your motivation is not going to help you be successful.

We rely so much on our motivation. We think that if we want it bad enough, we'll just do it. We've already covered this fallacy in the last chapter when we talked about the myth that your vision needs to be more than your why.

And your productivity is based on more than just your motivation.

I had a conversation with a friend once that made me chuckle. She said to me, "I love how you map things out and make all these plans, but I just don't work like that. When I want to get something done, I just get motivated and do it—I don't need a list."

Well good for you, sweetie.

But here is the thing: there aren't a lot of people like that. And honestly, this friend is also a person who I see complain a *lot* about what doesn't get done around her home. She often posts on social media about how behind she is. And from the outside, it seems like her motivation doesn't strike a lot.

And that is *normal*.

We need to stop pretending like we're just going to be motivated all the time to do things. Because I don't know about you, but even as a driven person, I'm *tired*.

I end my days a bit drained from the mommy carpool and managing my home and the emotions of my family. I often really and truly want to be motivated to do things but just can't get started.

That is, unless I have a plan.

The Power of Your Plan

When I got my first Life Coach Certification (I have three— one as a general life coach, a certification in cognitive behavioral technique, and a certification in happiness— which is super fun to add to my toolbox), I was so excited.

I couldn't wait to become an official Certified Life Coach so that I could really dig in and help my moms in a way that would empower them to make long-term changes in their families and for themselves.

My motivation and my why were both super strong and I was pumped and couldn't wait to get started.

But it wasn't the only thing on my plate. So, by the time it came to the end of the day—which was when I had blocked out time to take lessons and get started on my goals—I just didn't want to.

It wasn't that I didn't want to help moms. It wasn't that I didn't want to learn and grow. And it wasn't that I was unmotivated or lazy. It was that I was a busy mom of three with a lot on my plate and exhausted by the end of the day.

And, after the third day in a row of not logging into my course to take the lessons I knew I needed to finish, I realized what was wrong. I was depending on my excitement for a goal to get me to accomplish it. See, the problem wasn't in my motivation—I had plenty. The problem was in my *plan*. I had thought that I would just sit down at the computer and be so dang pumped to learn that I would get started.

And some nights I did. Some nights, I grabbed my notebook and dove into learning. And other nights, I struggled to even open the computer instead of collapsing on the couch to watch *The Office*.

This was a huge turning point in how I taught productivity and how I changed my personal approach to it. Once I realized that I needed a tighter plan, I learned how I could have flexibility and a plan that would push me through when I didn't feel motivated.

And maybe you've been there: in a place where you want to accomplish your goals but feel overwhelmed or burnt out and don't know where to start.

I bet you were so excited to go through the first few chapters of this book and create a vision. Right now (if you've done the action items I shared at the end of each chapter), you're feeling excited for your goals. It's the same high you feel when you make your New Year's Resolutions.

And we know what's coming next.

The crash.

The excitement *is* going to fade. Your motivation will wane. You will have days where you won't hit your goals, and you'll want to quit.

It is okay.

Instead of getting frustrated with ourselves for that happening, we're going to spend the rest of the book creating a plan to work *around* the days you're not motivated. A plan that makes sense in your life as a busy mom.

And a plan that starts with just fifteen minutes at a time.

The Power of the 15 Minute Formula

After a few days of feeling like a failure because I wasn't digging into my life coaching course, I went back to the drawing board. I decided to stop waiting to "feel like doing it" and instead, make a plan that would be easy to follow when I was feeling unmotivated or tired.

That's exactly how the 15 Minute Formula was born.

What we're going to dissect in this book is how you can use fifteen-minute chunks of your day to make big gains on your goals. It's not about having three hours to work on a goal (I mean seriously, having three hours of free time as a mom is pretty unheard of) or trying to create routines overnight.

We're going to take everything and fit it into the power pockets of your day.

Because here is the thing about fifteen minutes: it's very easy to spend it scrolling Instagram or Facebook and can pass by super fast. But it's also easy to convince yourself to do even a tiny task since if it's only for fifteen minutes.

Now I know in the last sentence I said *only* fifteen minutes, but I want you to start to switch your mind about the word "only."

We often will toss fifteen minutes aside because it's "not enough time" to make perfect progress. That's a perfectionist mentality, and it's time to push that to the side.

Just because we can't do things perfectly or as perfectly as we picture them in our head does *not* mean it's not progress.

Showing up for your goals, even just fifteen minutes at a time *is* progress. If you create a plan like the one I'm going to show you that has you taking action in fifteen minutes a day, you might not feel like you're doing much. But give it time and the compound effect will kick in.

I first read about the concept of the compound effect in the book (with the same name) by Darren Hardy. In this book, he defines the compound effect as "the principle of reaping huge rewards from a series of small, smart choices."[2]

This was a game changer for me when it came to productivity. I come from a place of an all-or-nothing mindset. And well, small wins didn't seem enough for me.

But what's great about the fifteen-minute micro-wins that we'll be discussing in the rest of the book is, if I show up for the fifteen minutes I have planned, amazing! I can pat myself on the back and tell myself I'm doing a good job. I can convince myself to show up for fifteen minutes, even on days I don't want to because it's "just fifteen minutes."

Often, I also find that on most days, I'll do more than the fifteen minutes I planned. The fifteen minutes zooms by, and I get engrossed in a project and want to keep going. On those days, I celebrate myself for showing up extra, and it allows me to get ahead and build a buffer for days when life throws me curveballs and I'm unable to work on my goals.

As busy moms, we need to anchor into our small wins. We need to celebrate them. And we need to create plans around them. Adding up small wins over time is how I read fifty-two books a year. It's how I wrote this book. It's how I've been able to manage my family and my business and run my home. And it's how I can spend my days in ebbs of productivity and rest while ditching the mom guilt that makes me feel like I'm failing or not good enough.

Fifteen-minute wins allow me to cheer myself on and keep going. Fifteen-minute wins have also been the best way to get my family on board with new routines without a major revolt happening or me getting frustrated because no one loves the new color-coded chore chart I printed from Pinterest and just assumed everyone would follow.

In this next section of the book, we're going to stop relying on motivation and create a plan that will help you move ahead—fifteen minutes at a time.

Chapter 3 Action Steps

1. If you haven't already, make sure you head to www.the-15minuteformula.com/free to get the reading guide for this book. In it, it lists out how to complete this book in fifteen minutes a day. Go into your planner and schedule out fifteen minutes a day, five days a week to read and take action on this book. Map your fifteen minutes out so we can do this together!

PILLAR #2

PRODUCTIVITY AND TIME MANAGEMENT

Chapter 4

Creating a Time-Blocked Schedule

Ten years ago, If I could have married my hourly planner, I would have done it.

I was in love. I was obsessed. I felt like I didn't know how to live without my days planned out minute by minute.

And that made sense—sort of.

I was a high school special education teacher, which meant I was everywhere. No exaggeration, there was one year where I was in a different classroom every single period—and sometimes multiple classrooms per period. I had to manage my caseload of students, attend IEP meetings, do push-in support for their regular education classrooms, teach my own resource room period, and on top of all of that, I was the lead teacher for ninth grade while running our student leadership program. If I didn't have my time mapped out by the half hour, I could potentially be in the wrong place at the wrong time.

When I left teaching to go full time into network marketing (which was two years before I started A Purpose Driven Mom), I thought that in order to be successful, I would need to do the same things. I had equated success with overplanning, being everywhere all the time, and scheduling myself from the minute I got up until the minute I got to bed, which was way too late most nights since I was getting up at 4 a.m. to "get it all done."

I had taken this mentality from teaching into motherhood, and I quickly learned that kids, well they don't give a rip about your schedule or your planner. (I know, how dare they!?)

I was trying to get my family onto a detailed, minute-by-minute schedule, and they weren't going with my plan, which led me to feel frustrated and resentful. I mean, didn't they know that I had a reason they needed to have their shoes on by 9:36 a.m. every day? (Oh, and that reason was that I was trying to control everything . . .)

Fast forward a few years, I was about to have my son and jump into productivity and life coaching and leave network marketing. I knew that I needed to do something different with my time management because being a time tyrant wasn't working for me or my family.

That was the first time I really and truly gave time blocking a try, and I haven't looked back.

How Time Blocking Gives You Freedom and Structure

I was so afraid to get started with time blocking because I thought that if I didn't have things mapped out to the minute, we'd get behind or something wouldn't get done. I couldn't have been farther from the truth.

Time blocking gave me the best of both worlds: freedom and structure.

If you're someone who wants more of a tight schedule, time blocking can work for you. If creating a schedule at all gives you hives and you want to be more go-with-the-flow, time blocking can work for you as well.

Time blocking allows you to have urgency by indicating what things need to get done at the end of the block—instead of just saying, "I'll get to it sometime today." And while you'll have urgency for each block, when you use the 15 Minute Formula system for time blocking (which I've named the Time Blocking Blueprint), you'll also get the freedom to decide what happens when, which is something we need as moms. We need to be flexible—because kids and their needs are unpredictable—while still having urgency to finish what's on our list.

The concept behind time blocking is simple: you create blocks of your day around events instead of going hour by hour. After working with hundreds of moms, I realized that while the concept is great, there are a few things you need to do to set your time blocks up for success.

How to Set Up Your Time Blocks

First things first—you have to set up your blocks. Grab the planner of your choice (or go to www.the15minuteformula. com/free to get the blank templates that go along with the 30-Day Action Guide) so that you can use a pencil and some highlighters and get messy with this process.

You're going to anchor your blocks around your day, and I suggest starting with events that are already taking place. This could be if you have a certain time to pick up or drop off your kids at school or sports, you go into work at a specific time, or even mealtimes if you eat around the same time each day.

You'll want your blocks to be between two and five hours total. If you have blocks that are less than two hours, you can fall into the trap of hourly scheduling, and if you go over five hours, you might struggle with the urgency piece of time blocking.

Quick note—you do *not* need to have the same blocks each day. You can have Monday/Wednesday/Friday blocks and Tuesday/Thursday blocks depending on the activities that day. You can make a separate block for the weekends or times when your partner might be traveling for work. Our lives are not the same each day, so there is no rule saying our blocks have to be.

Here's an example of how I might separate my time blocks. We'll use this example for each step of creating your blocks.

6:00 a.m. – 9:00 a.m. (from wake up until preschool drop off)

9:00 a.m. – 12:00 p.m. (while kids are at preschool)

12:00 p.m. – 3:00 p.m. (from lunch until nap time ends)

3:00 p.m. – 7:00 p.m. (from wake up until bedtime)

7:00 p.m. – 11:00 p.m. (kids' bedtime until mom bedtime)

As you see in this example, I've created blocks around events that naturally happen in the day such as nap or meals. You'll also notice that the blocks go back-to-back with no gaps in between. We'll address that later in the chapter when we talk about transition time.

Creating Themes for Your Blocks

Once you've got your blocks set up, it's time to create themes for each one. Theming each block is going to be key to your productivity and using the 15 Minute Formula for your routines and goals. There is a reason this chapter is coming before we break your goals down—if you have a good handle on your schedule and your time, it becomes super easy to plop in when you'll work on goals, projects, home routines, and more.

We're going to make general themes for each of your blocks based on what makes sense for you and your home. These themes are going to be around the roles that we identified in previous chapters when we talked about creating your micro priorities. (You did that, right?) Your themes are going to be loosely laid categories that will enable you to figure out where to put what when you make your schedule.

Let's look at that example and add some themes to it.

6:00 a.m. – 9:00 a.m. self-care and Mommy

9:00 a.m. – 12:00 p.m. home management

12:00 p.m. – 3:00 p.m. Mommy time

3:00 p.m. – 7:00 p.m. family time

7:00 p.m. – 11:00 p.m. personal and relationship time

Let's break all this down and what it actually means when it comes to the themes.

6:00 a.m. – 9:00 a.m. self-care and Mommy

This is before the kids get up and while they get ready for their day. This is when Mom can work on some of her personal self-care (like workout or Bible study) and help get the kids out the door.

9:00 a.m. – 12:00 p.m. home management

With the kids at preschool, this is the block when errands, phone calls, cleaning, or other projects get done. If this was a work-at-home mom, this could be where she chunks out her work time.

12:00 p.m. – 3:00 p.m. Mommy time

Kids are home from school, and it's time for lunch and a nap for the youngest. While he naps, you're on Mommy time with your other child where you play, read, and spend time together.

3:00 p.m. – 7:00 p.m. family time

Everyone is up, and it's time to get ready for dinner, maybe a family walk, game, or TV show. This is also a great time to have everyone complete the nighttime routines or pickups from the day.

7:00 p.m. – 11:00 p.m. personal and relationship time

Kiddos are in bed, and it's a great time to work on your personal goals, spend time with your partner, on a Zoom with some girlfriends, or curling up with a book or your Netflix binge of choice.

The key to your themes is that being able to go back and anchor into your vision for the block. Not only do you have an idea of what you'd like to happen when, but you can start to ditch the guilt. Instead of feeling like you're putting off that sink full of dishes for the day, you know that you can play with your kids now since you have time in the schedule at a later time to get it done.

This helped me so much as I worked from home when my kids were not in school. Right now, they go to school all day, but I built my business with them all three home, then one part-time at school, two part-time at school, and now all three are in full-day school—so I know what it's like to have to juggle it all. When it was "work block," we created norms in my home where my kids knew that right now is "Mommy work time" and later will be "Mommy time" where we can get to play. It helped me to ditch the mom guilt that creeps up or that feeling like I had to have my house perfectly clean to start working because I knew I had time planned later.

Theming time blocks is what attracted Pamela, one of my clients, to the 15 Minute Formula. As a busy, working mom, everything shifted for her when the pandemic of 2020 hit, and all of a sudden, everyone was home. Once we went over how to make blocks thematic, a light bulb went off in her head.

She needed to work, but she also needed to manage her home and kids. Working from home created a lot of guilt about when she should be working, how much time she should spend with her kids, and how much housework needed to get done during the day.

Once she created time blocks with themes that made sense for her, she talked them through with her husband and was realistic about how much time she needed each day to work. She was able to ask for help (which we know is super tricky for us moms) and focus on work when it was a work block and home when it was a home block.

She was also able to customize a schedule based on her kid's energy. She started to notice when her kids were more squirrely (you know that time of 4–6 p.m.?) and made the themes for these blocks work for them instead of just trying to stick to the schedule. That customization made time blocks work for Pamela because she didn't feel boxed into a schedule but instead had the freedom to make it work in her home—whatever that looked like!

When creating your blocks, they won't be perfect. Permission to be imperfect and make mistakes granted!

Some things will happen outside of "their block," some activities will spill into another block, and some days will be a hot mess. It's okay. We're not going after perfection here. We're working on intention. If you create your vision and use your micro priorities to make an *intentional* schedule, you'll notice things will start to fall into place much easier.

The Three Plans You Need to Make

Once you have your theme, it can be pretty tempting to jump in and toss everything into your blocks.

Let's slow down a second.

I have an entire chapter dedicated to the concept of routine and habit stacking later on in the book, but I want to pause to remind you of something:

You don't have to do it all right away.

And by shoving *way* too much into your schedule and onto your plate, you're setting yourself up for feelings of burnout, overwhelm, and resentment.

The world tells us that we have to go-go-go and do-do-do. That if we're not performing at a million miles an hour at all times, then we are failing.

I'm here to remind you that "the world" isn't one of your priorities. "The world" doesn't know you, your family, or your unique season of life or situation. *"The world" is not in charge of your schedule and productivity—you are.*

By slowing down and creating a plan for your time blocks with steady growth instead of jumping in and trying to do it all right away, you're going to create lifelong habits and routines for not just you but your kids and family as well.

And that's why I'm going to suggest instead of making one plan where you toss all the things in, you create three separate plans that allow you to have room for growth and room for life to happen and toss you a curveball or two.

These three will be

- Your Ideal Plan
- Your In-Progress Plan
- Your When-the-Poop-Hits-the-Fan Plan

Your Ideal Plan

This is the plan where your vision will be held. You'll hear me say a lot that we need to start with the end in mind, and that's where vision comes in and the reason we covered it first when discussing the 15 Minute Formula.

If you don't know where you want to go, it'll be really hard to make plans for anything. When you have a vision for each plan, you'll most likely surpass your goals early.

A vision will become the anchor for you when it comes to growth and planning.

Make a copy of each plan you made (in case you have one for each day or something different for the weekends or when you're away, etc.), and let's break down where you want each plan to go.

Inside your ideal plans, write down your dream day. What routines would you like to have in play? Where do you have time for rest and fun? When are you working on your goals? By creating this vision now, you can create your plan for the future and how to use routine stacking. Let's break down an ideal day based on the plans we created in the previous example.

6:00 a.m. – 9:00 a.m. self-care and Mommy
Bible reading and meditation
Workout
Breakfast time
Shower and dress
Kids' morning chores
9:00 a.m. – 12:00 p.m. home management
Run errands
Any phone calls
Daily Cleaning
Work on home project
12:00 p.m. – 3:00 p.m. Mommy time
Lunch
Reading time

Outside play

Games and activities

3:00 p.m. – 7:00 p.m. family time

Play date or kid's activity

Dinner

Family devotional

Family walk

Kids' tablet time

Family game or movie

Nightly closeout

7:00 p m – 11:00 p.m. personal and relationship time

Evening pick up and routine

Personal course lesson or reading

Show with hubby

Bed

You can be as detailed as you want with each day or give a quick summary. In your ideal day routines, you now have a vision for where you want your plans to go—even if they aren't there yet.

Your In-Progress Plan

The ideal vision we created in the last example was great—but whew, it was *jam packed.* And if you are new to routines and time blocking, there is a high likelihood that you don't have your days this together.

And that's okay.

That's why we're now going to create your in-progress plan.

Your in-progress plan will be ever growing, your place to track how things are going at the moment. Instead of trying to recreate your ideal plans on day one, I want to encourage you to pick either one plan to start with or one task in each plan.

This will allow you to slowly make the routines happen without getting overwhelmed. Each week, you'll pick a new piece of your plan to stack onto the previous week—and prevent what I like to call the "Monday Mentality."

The Monday Mentality is probably familiar to you.

Have you ever tried to lose weight? Yeah, me too. And as human beings, we tend to follow the same pattern. We make this super intense plan where we vow to go to the gym for two hours a day, never look at chocolate or sniff a carb. By Wednesday (if we're lucky), we're so overwhelmed that we just give up and tell ourselves we'll start again on Monday.

Hence the name, the "Monday Mentality."

You'll start to see this pattern over and over again in so much that you do. It is one of the reasons we make the same resolutions year after year and our vision boards contain similar pictures as our life goes on.

We're trying to do too much, too fast.

For your ideal plans, create a plan that allows you to build on what is working and slowly add to it. You can add something each week, each month, or every other day if you want. But I highly suggest you don't try to do it all right away.

By having an in-progress plan, you'll be able to grow at your own pace with what makes sense for your season. And, since you've created your ideal plan and vision, if you want to change your pace, it's easy to do because you know what else you want to accomplish in the future.

In order to determine where to start with each plan, ask yourself a few questions:

Which task(s) in each plan would make the most difference for me at this moment?

Which task(s) am I looking forward to trying to accomplish or work on?

Which task(s) makes the most sense to work on based on my season?

By going through this process each week and as you add things to your plans, you can use the priority-based productivity concept to customize your plans based on your needs.

Here is an example of an in-progress plan for someone just starting out. In parentheses I put what the thought process might be for why that person chose each task.

Week 1 Focus:

6:00 a.m. – 9:00 a.m. self-care and Mommy

Workout *(I know if I don't get a workout in for me, I am low energy, so I want to make sure this gets done first thing.)*

9:00 a.m. – 12:00 p.m. home management

Work on home project *(I have big goals to clean my house, but there is so much clutter that I know I have to focus on my decluttering project before getting to the cleaning, so decluttering comes first.)*

12:00 p.m. – 3:00 p.m. Mommy time

Lunch *(I want to focus on healthier options for the kids, so I'm going to work on menu planning lunch this week.)*

3:00 p.m. – 7:00 p.m. family time

Family walk *(Our lives are getting so busy, and I really want us to spend more time together. I know if I don't plan it, it won't happen.)*

7:00pm—11:00 p.m. personal and relationship time

Evening pick up and routine *(I know if I get my evening pick up done, I can be less stressed in the morning, so I'll start here.)*

As you can see, the rationale for where to start in each plan makes sense for their micro priorities, and that is key! Now, when the next week comes, she can decide whether she wants to add something to the in-progress plan or keep it the same.

Note: You don't have to add something to each plan each week. Maybe in week two, you only add something to one plan because you are still working to be consistent with the other ones. That is totally fine—your pace and your rules!

How do you know if you're ready to add to a plan?

There are a few factors you can look at to determine whether you're ready to stack your plan.

1. **Data.** I suggest tracking your progress each week to see how you're actually doing and not just guess. This allows you to take the emotions out and not assign feelings of being "lazy" or "bad" to yourself, and be a detective about your plan.

    If you don't hit your goal for the week data wise, you can instead stack your frequency. I never suggest planning anything for seven days a week—you're just setting yourself up for failure. Instead plan for five days and those two extra are a bonus.

    But say you do plan to complete your evening routine five out of five days, and in the first week, you only hit two of those five days. Instead of tossing the goal out the window completely or adding more to a routine that isn't really consistent yet, I suggest you add a frequency stack. Okay, you didn't hit five out of five days, but for this next week, can you aim for four out of five or three out of five? This will allow you to make progress and grow while also being realistic and not overwhelming yourself.

2. **Seasonality and feeling.** I want you to look at the data first to try to make nonemotional decisions

around your plans, but before you decide to add more to any plans, make sure it makes sense.

Do you have a busy week coming up? Are you traveling or out of town? Is there a work project or additional goals that need your attention? It may not make sense for you to stack this week, even if you hit your goal.

Give yourself permission and grace to move at a slower pace so it can stick. If you decide to add something to each plan on week two because you did amazingly week one but forget that it's the first week of back to school and there are meetings and sports and a ton of paperwork you need to do, you're most likely going to get overwhelmed and want to stop.

Take a pause before you add to your routine stacks and ask yourself, "Does this make sense or am I just adding because I feel like I'm supposed to?"

When-the-Poop-Hits-the-Fan Plan

I'm a mom of three—of course I was going to talk about poop at some point in this book!

Just kidding, we're not switching gears into a potty-training book, but I do want to talk about poop—or at least the days when the poop hits the fan.

When you get started with time blocking, it can feel so exciting—you're ready to go. But what do you do on the days when someone gets sick, distractions toss you off course, or you just need a mental health break?

If we're not proactive about our time, these types of days will easily throw us and our goals off course. So, while we're working on your ideal plan and your in-progress plan, let's create a third.

This is your contingency plan. This is your back up for the days you want to rip your hair out.

When the pandemic of 2020 tossed everything around, we as moms had to learn to pivot and be flexible. When school started up again in the fall, I was fortunate that my kids' preschool was open. That meant that they would be able to go to school barring any COVID-19 outbreaks.

And while this time was so unpredictable for all of us, I realized something. At some point in the year, they would most likely be sent home from either themselves getting sick, a classmate, or a staff member. I also knew that if I got the call that they were home for a week or longer out of the blue, it had the potential to completely throw me off and that I would struggle to adapt fast.

Before they went to school, I decided that while I won't know exactly when they will get sent home, I wanted to be prepared for it just in case. So, I made a plan for it in advance.

I used my current plans to identify how I would move my work-from-home schedule around (because Mama still needed to work), what my kids would be doing during that time, and how we'd have Mommy school and activities at home. During the year, every time the teacher emailed over any type of worksheet, I would print it out and put it in the filing cabinet to use as a backup plan. I created a Trello board full of resources and activities that I could use.

Because I knew this, I would be fine and adapt to having them home. I'm Mom, I've got this. But it would stress me out to have to pull it together last minute, and that stress would lead me to being short with my kids. So instead of setting myself up for failure, I decided to prepare for it and give future me a present in the form of an already done schedule and handful of activities we could do at a moment's notice.

While we don't know exactly what is going to pop up at any moment, by creating at least one general when-the-poop-hits-the-fan plan, you at least have something you can customize for the situation.

In order to do this, look at your ideal plan and ask yourself, "If I could *only* do one thing per plan, what would it be?" This way, you still have a focus of getting at least the bare minimum done to take care of you, your home, and your family without trying to jam in a million things when things feel like they are falling apart a bit. Doing this in advance is a great way to set yourself up to still stay as on top of your goals as you can while not adding as much stress to your plate.

Here is an example from the ideal day that we created at the start of this chapter. In parentheses is an explanation of why these things were chosen. And remember, that's the best part—you can customize it for what *you* need to feel successful that day!

6:00 a.m. – 9:00 a.m. self-care and Mommy

Shower and dress *(By getting dressed for the day, I'll feel a little bit better about the day and myself.)*

9:00 a.m. – 12:00 p.m. home management

Daily cleaning *(Keeping on top of my daily cleaning task will help me not feel behind tomorrow.)*

12:00 p.m. – 3:00 p.m. mommy time

Lunch *(We gotta eat, am I right? And I know on hard days, I can forget to take care of myself and eat.)*

3:00 p.m. – 7:00 p.m. family time

Family devotional *(Today may be hard, but having our family together centered in the Word will help us focus on what matters, not the stress of the day.)*

7:00pm—11:00 p.m. personal and relationship time

Evening pick up and routine *(Keeping to my nighttime pick up will ensure that tomorrow I'm not starting the day feeling behind. Tomorrow is a new day!)*

As you can see in this example, a lot got taken off the day. And on days when someone is sick or your family is having a tough time, just getting lunch can feel like a miracle. Now, even if the tablet is in charge all day or you spend it binge watching *Gilmore Girls*, at least you got the bare minimum you needed accomplished to feel better about the day while not getting super behind on other things.

A Note About Rest

It's easy as a mom to run yourself into the ground and burn out.

I know. I've been there.

So, let's pause for a quick reminder.

You don't have to earn rest. It's not a reward. It's something you need and something you deserve.

If you're feeling awful and even your when-the-poop-hits-the-fan schedule doesn't happen that day—THAT IS OKAY.

You don't owe it to anyone to prove you were productive. You don't have to keep pushing even when you're feeling awful.

By taking care of you, you're doing your family a favor. I'm sure you've heard the phrase, "You can't pour from an empty cup" (which has been credited to people like Joseph Flemming and Norm Kelly), and it's true. By continuing to push and push and push, you're setting yourself up for burnout and resentment.

The reason I suggest you make this contingency schedule for when things are a mess is because I know that for many of us moms, those days that feel all over the place are the days that we don't know how to come back from. They are the days where we toss our goals for the month out the window. The days when we just want to quit.

By proactively making a plan just in case, you're doing your future self a service and helping her out.

But permission granted to not do anything on the days when you just can't and the days when you just need to rest and refuel (either physically or mentally). And make sure when you're making your ideal plans, you've set aside some time for rest each week in advance. This will help limit the burnout in the long run.

Chapter 4 Action Steps

1. Craft out your three plans: ideal, in-progress, and when-the-poop-hits-the-fan.
2. Create themes around these plans.
3. Figure out how you want to grow your plans.

Chapter 5

Additional Blocks to Add Into Your Day

Key Mini Blocks to Add Into Your Day

As I started to adapt time blocking into my life, I came across some major hiccups.

What happens when something is supposed to take five minutes, and it actually takes twenty? What do you do if you don't want to stop an activity, but the time block is ending? And how do you play catch up when you forget something or a task pops up midweek?

In this section, I want to talk about three mini blocks that I add inside of my bigger time blocks that allow for things to run smoother and for life to "just happen."

Using Transition Time to Make Things Smoother

During the pandemic of 2020, our routines went wild. Like pretty much everyone else's family, we had to navigate huge changes and figure out how to make things work.

And the biggest one was that now, my husband and I were both working from home with the kids.

My husband is a school administrator, so you can imagine the level of work and stress on his plate during this time. Toss three of our kids now being home full time while I was trying to work and grow my business, and it was a recipe for disaster and miscommunicated expectations.

As the control freak—ahem, I mean *organized person*—that I am, I thought that if I just remade our schedules, we'd be fine. I created a beautiful chart, reworked our routines, and found time for both me and my husband to have at least two hours a day alone in the office to get focused work done. We knew that with these changes, we'd have to learn how to navigate work around them, but if we could each have a small window of time where we could "be at work," we'd be more efficient and feel less frustrated.

And then . . . day one hit.

My block of work time was from 8:00 a.m.–10:00 a.m., so promptly at eight, I marched into the office for my work time. I was excited to work with focus and honestly wasn't too concerned with what was happening in the other room. At ten o'clock on the dot, I closed my computer, marched into the other room, and loudly proclaimed that "I was done working and it was time for Mommy school." (Since I have preschoolers, I opted for a version of homeschool instead of getting on virtual classes while they were home. As a former teacher, I really enjoyed doing this, but it sure did feel like a lot of pressure on me to "do it all"—but we'll talk more about that later in the book.)

To my dismay, no one else seemed ready for me. In my head, my two hours would be up and they would be ready to move to the next block. But what I imagined in my head did not translate because I never communicated it.

So instead of doing the rational thing, I got irritated. I stomped around, mumbling under my breath about how I have to "do everything," and I shouldn't "have to" facilitate pick up because it wasn't my turn to be in charge. (Oh, don't look at me like that, you know you've been there!)

When I started to dig into my feelings, I felt irritated and honestly annoyed that no one was respecting my perfect schedule. But in reality, I didn't set the tone so that we could implement this perfect schedule with success. Instead of staying in reactive mode, I decided to brainstorm some ways to be proactive and communicate the routine better (that is, after I was done huffing and puffing).

Around this time, I realized what was missing—and that was transition time.

Remember when you were in high school and the bell rang to signal class was over? You'd have four minutes to grab your stuff, run across the building, high five a friend, and get to class. As you entered that new class, your brain started to shift from Algebra to History, and you were ready to start a new period.

We need to start bringing this same concept into our schedules.

Transition time is helpful for not only us but our kids. If you have ever witnessed a mega tantrum because you realized it was bedtime and pulled your kids from their activity to go right to bed, you know what I mean.

Transition and routine help kids feel safe and see predictability. It allows their brains to recognize something is changing and that they need to prepare for something new. When you add transitions into your blocks, you'll notice that things move smoother and kids are more willing to change from activity to activity.

Ways to Add Transition Time Into Your Blocks

Transition time can be anywhere from five to fifteen minutes and added between any activity. Think of these transitions as a reset button and a signal that it's time to change.

Here are some of my favorite transitions to add in:

A Quick Pick Up

I love a good fifteen-minute pick up. We do these multiple times throughout our day as a transition, and it helps make the end of the night so much easier. If you're changing blocks and the kids have toys out, it's a clear transition that it's time to clean up. If you're moving from dinner to the after-dinner block, putting on a timer and having everyone help pick up the meal or do a quick sweep of the floor can not only help get things picked up faster but act as a closing time of the block.

Snack Time

Snack time is a natural transition from block to block. When we were moving from my work block to Mommy school block, we would combine a quick pick up and snack before changing activities. This allowed me to get my materials ready but also refueled my tiny people so they weren't hangry as we went into the next block.

Movement

Here is another idea taken from my days in the classroom: adding movement into your block can be a great transition for both you and the kiddos. (And a quick disclaimer, I suggest you add transitions into each block whether you are doing it for yourself or the kids. We all can benefit from them!)

Movement gives us time to stretch our bodies and clear our heads, and it is a great way to get out any extra energy that you might need to get rid of. For my kids, I might put on the Go Noodle app on the TV and let them run and dance around, find the *Trolls* soundtrack on YouTube or Spotify, or take a quick walk around the block.

Reflection

I know we've covered great transition activities to add into your kids' days, but let's not forget about you. Reflection practices throughout your day are a great transition for you and the kids and allow you to take a pause when you need it.

We often are barreling through life and only stop when we hit a place of burn out. Instead, let's add in some intentional reflection as a transition at least once a day. This can be pausing to formally add a line to your gratitude journal, practicing mindfulness while doing a check-in with how you're feeling, or taking five minutes outside to pray, meditate, or sit in quiet.

My suggestion is to be proactive about adding transition times in. Create a list of your family's favorite transition activities and keep it on the fridge as a reminder. Pick which ones make the most sense in your day and give them a try. You'll soon find yourself getting in a flow and realizing at what time Mommy needs a five-minute time out and reflection and what time of day you need a family dance party to get the wiggles out!

A Note About Time

Just a quick reminder that the 15 Minute Formula is all about not using an hourly schedule to micromanage your day; it's about the freedom and flexibility that completing tasks in reasonable chunks can give you. That being said, if your transition activity moves a block from ending at 10:00 to 10:15, that's okay. If your family is having fun with movement or in a groove with a pick up, it's more than okay if it goes "over time."

Remember, we're aiming to help you release the control of having everything line up perfectly and instead be empowered to make decisions to prioritize and customize your family's day!

Creating Buffer Time

On top of adding in transition time to your blocks, I am also going to suggest you add in what I call buffer time. Buffer time is perfect for those mornings that feel wonky on the way out the door, when you're running late because you can't find something, or your people are just moving at a snail's pace.

Buffer time gives you exactly that—a buffer.

A common mistake I notice moms making when they create their schedules is that they add in *way* too much stuff.

Can I let you in on a little secret?

You do not have to add something to every hour of your schedule and your planner.

By adding in too much stuff, you're setting that schedule of yours up to implode. If every minute is scheduled (and remember, now that you're a time-blocking wizard, you're not going to schedule like that anyway, right?), what do you do when things run off course?

Because here is the thing: we know they will! We know that something is going to run over, or we will not have saved enough time for something we need to get done.

Enter buffer time!

In order to create an actual buffer, you need to know where you're starting, and that is where a time inventory comes in. A time inventory is a place where you can track what and how you're spending your time. The goal of our inventory is to be a detective of your time; it isn't to shame you or make you feel like you're lazy or wasting time.

We either underestimate or overestimate how long a task will take. In order to adequately create buffer time, you'll want to know exactly how long something takes.

To work on a time inventory, pick out three to five days in the next week that you'll track your tasks (and if you want a printable version of a time inventory, head over to www.the15minutesformula.com to get the free resources). You can track this on paper (see below for an example) or even in the notes app of your phone. No need to get fancy here—remember the goal is to be a time detective.

During this time, write down all the things you're doing and make sure to include how long you're working on them. You can write a start and stop time or simply start the timer on your phone and track when you're done. Don't get too caught up in being to the minute, even a close estimate is better than nothing.

When you're done, you'll be able to grab some highlighters and categorize tasks (which will help a ton with your time blocks) and see exactly how long something takes.

Time inventory

TIME	TIME SPENT	TASK	CATEGORY	NOTES

What Do You Do with This Data?

Once you have the numbers, there are a few ways you can use them to create buffer time.

1. Make sure you're not adding in too much to your blocks.

Since you have a good estimate of how long something is going to take, when you create your blocks, make sure you're not jamming too much in. Once you've mapped out your in-progress plan, add in twenty extra minutes of nothing. If you can't add twenty minutes without going into the next block, you have *too* much planned for that block. See if you can take something away or move it to another time.

2. Use it as motivation when you're not feeling like getting into action.

Since I've done a time inventory, I know it takes approximately six minutes to unload my dishwasher. But I can spend a good twenty minutes (or more) complaining about doing it.

When I'm really not feeling like getting myself into gear, I reference my inventory to remind myself that it won't take that long. I use a positive statement such as "This will only take me six minutes and then I can go back to relaxing" to help reframe my attitude about getting started.

3. Notice your common distractors.

When doing a time inventory, I suggest you have your most common distractors simply listed at the bottom of the page. These could be things like checking email, scrolling Facebook, or pinning things on Pinterest. Throughout the day, whenever you notice you are doing them, just put a tally mark next to it instead of tracking it minute by minute.

At the end of the inventory, it will most likely be eye opening how often you are getting distracted, and then you can use that data to create a proactive plan around it.

For example, if you notice that you are checking email thirty times a day (friend, this is no joke. After a few days I noticed just how much I was opening my inbox and getting distracted on my tasks), you might want to take the app off your phone for a week and decide to only check it when you're on the desktop.

I also did this with my social media. I used to love Facebook, but honestly, it's probably my least favorite place currently. People are nasty and rude, and it doesn't provide me much value. Besides my community groups, which I love, I realized Facebook was making me irritated and annoyed. I also was checking it *all* the time—at the traffic light, during dinner, in the bathroom, etc. I knew something had to change, so I started with taking it off my phone on the weekends, and it became *so* nice. At first it was hard to not have it, but I told myself I could always just check on my computer if I really wanted to get on. It's still a practice I do to this day, and it allows me to unplug and be more present with my family and less annoyed at others.

Ending the Stop and Drop

If you're a busy mom, I know the demands of your family can take its toll. Everyone seems to always need you, and sometimes they expect you to just drop everything because they forgot something they need for school or a craft item for a project.

Have no fear—we're about to end all that.

See, I used to be the queen of pleasing people. I liked the feeling I got when I played the martyr in my home, and looking back now, I can admit that. Being stressed out and running all over gave me purpose and meaning and made me feel like I was a "good mom" because I would put all of my tasks aside for my family.

And then I burnt out.

Resentment started to creep back in, and I started to feel unappreciated and wondered when I was supposed to have time for what I wanted to get done in between the random Target runs and grocery pickups. And on top of it, I was creating a bad habit of enabling my family and teaching them that they could be last minute about things because "Mommy's got it."

I didn't realize this was even a problem until the day my then twelve-year-old ran out of deodorant. It seemed like a simple enough request from him: "Hey, I need deodorant. Can you get me some today at the store?" But something clicked in my head.

So, I said "no."

Now if you're someone who struggles to say no to your family or anyone in general, I really want you to zone back into what I'm saying here.

Saying no to our kids isn't a bad thing. It can actually be a gift.

I realized that I had taught him that as soon as he needed something, I would stop and drop what I was doing and jump to the rescue. I was doing this all over my house. My husband needed something for a meal, I'd run to the store. One of the kids forgot about something they needed for school; bye bye, plan for the day. I'd run and grab it. One time, my oldest needed an all-white outfit for his World Percussion presentation and told me the night before. I spent two hours trying to find a pair of white pants that fit him at 9 p.m. on a Sunday—I told you, it was bad.

I decided that day that enough was enough. We needed to make some changes, create and respect boundaries, and fix things so that I wasn't running all over all the time.

And that's how thought catcher time was born.

Thought catcher time is another block I highly suggest you add into your week because it will save you time and brain space.

The premise of thought catcher time is simple: block out one to two 30-minute spaces a week of nothing. Yup. Leave it completely blank. I know it might feel tough, but resist the urge to fill it up just because the blank space is there.

Your planner will not spontaneously combust because you didn't fill up every line. Promise.

Even though you'll spend Sunday making a plan for the week (and we'll talk about the weekly planning system in Chapter 14), there will still be things you'll forget.

Have you ever been in the shower (where the best ideas come, of course), and a million things run through your brain? Or how about when you try to go to bed and your to-do list seems to grow with every minute?

Instead of freaking out over when these things are going to happen or dropping everything in the moment, you're going to use your thought catcher time to get it done.

See the thing is, we know stuff is going to pop up. We know that we'll forget about the phone calls and paperwork that we were supposed to do. We can predict that at some point during the week, something we didn't plan for needs to get done.

So, let's be proactive about it instead of reactive.

Thought catcher time is a proactive strategy to allow yourself to plan for distraction, curve balls, and things that just pop up. You won't know each week what is going to pop up, but at least now you've got the time to handle it.

Because if you don't create the time to handle the things that will pop up, those things will push the other things you've preplanned off your schedule. So now, when random things pop in your head, I want you to create a list—and not take action (unless it's a true emergency).

There are rarely things that are true emergencies that need us to stop right away to do them. I want you to start respecting the you from Sunday who made this great plan for the week and stop adding things to today's schedule. Ninety-nine percent of the things you think of today will be fine if they get done tomorrow or later in the week. It's time to stop living in a state of urgency and rush, and create boundaries for your time.

I have a section in my planner where I keep my thought catcher ideas, but you can get a Post-it note, use a whiteboard, or keep them in your phone. Designate one place to list all the random thoughts and ideas. And then, during your predetermined thought catcher time, you can work on them.

For me, I have a thirty-minute block on Wednesday mornings and a thirty-minute block on Friday afternoons. I've predetermined that on Wednesdays after I drop my kids off, I will head over to Target to run any of the errands I need to run. I then sit in my car and make any of the phone calls that I need to make. When my thirty minutes are up, I head home, and whatever didn't get done can now get *planned out* for next week.

My thirty-minute block on Friday afternoons is my designated admin time. I keep a list all week of random paperwork, bills, or house things I need to handle, and I do them all Friday after school when we're all relaxing from the school week. This allows me to not feel like I have to panic and get frantic to get things done but stay calm and in control because, even though it has to get done, I know I have created space in advance to do it.

By creating thought catcher time, not only will you be respecting your own boundaries but you'll start to teach your family how to respect them too. If you're coming from a place of "stop and drop," it may take your family some time to get used to this.

"What do you mean you're not going to get this for me as soon as I say it?"

And while your kids might not say that, if you have a teen like me, I'm sure you're picturing a great eye roll and mumble under their breath.

During these moments, it's key to have a conversation with your family about this so they can understand the new boundary and what to expect. It could sound something like this

"So, I know Mom used to be able to stop and do things right away, but I'm trying something new where I go to the store less. If you need something, please ask me! But know that I run my errands on Wednesday and Friday, and you'll have to wait until then to get it."

"But, Mom! I'm out of deodorant, and today's Monday! Are you saying I have to wait two days??"

"Yup, I am. But I'm sure we can find someone else's around the house you can use for now. In the future, if you notice that it's getting low, please make sure to ask in advance or put it on the shopping list."

Now I'm not saying they'll smile and nod and just go along with you right away. What I am saying is that it's up to you as mom to create a culture in your home. A culture where mom isn't the martyr. A culture where mom isn't resentful about doing it all. A culture where mom feels respected and your kids learn more personal responsibility.

And by adding in this tiny thought catcher time into your week, you'll start making moves toward this culture you hope to create.

Chapter 5 Action Items

1. Go back to the in-progress plans you mapped out in the last chapter.
2. Pencil in thought catcher time for the next week.
3. Brainstorm a list of transition activities you'll start using.
4. Start a time inventory so you can accurately make more buffer time in your days.

Chapter 6

Productivity Hacks to Amplify Your Blocks

Did you know our brains are not actually meant to multitask?

Our brains prefer to do a single task. It's what all the productivity gurus and scientific studies share. And I believe it—being able to have one focused hour on a task will lend me to getting more done than trying to do multiple things at one time.

But I'm also a mom. And a realist. And while I think you should try to do a single task as much as possible, I know it's not our reality.

If you've ever been in the kitchen around 4:30 p.m., you know exactly what I'm talking about.

It's time to get dinner going, and everyone just got settled in from school or after-school activities. You're trying to get bookbags put away and lunch containers in the sink. Your kids want to play, need to do homework, and are trying to get your attention. The sink is overloaded from earlier in the day, you need some free hands to stir up dinner, and you just don't know what to do.

Hello. Welcome to motherhood.

If you've ever been in that spot, you know how nice it would be to not have to multitask, but let's get real: it's near impossible most days, at least for an extended period of time.

Focused Tasking with the 15 Minute Formula

Instead of trying to set aside two hours to focus on one project, let's talk about how you can do what I call focused tasking with the 15 Minute Formula.

Because here is the thing that I know: we will use the fact that we can't do a single task as a procrastination tool. We cling to the fact that "oh well, I don't have an hour to focus on this goal" as a reason to put off our goals, dreams, and even completion of day-to-day tasks.

So, let's change our thinking around it. Let's start a single task in just fifteen minutes at a time.

I had a big goal of getting my house decluttered. We just had So. Much. Stuff. I was drowning in all the things, and I knew that if I could get rid of things, it would clear up space in not just my house but also my head.

I put this goal off for months. Each month, I would say I would get started, but unless I had the perfect time, the perfect environment, and all the stars aligned, I wouldn't do it. I had gotten it in my head that if I didn't have a full Saturday free to declutter, there was no point in even starting.

Maybe you've been there too?

This type of procrastination is actually rooted in perfectionism. We don't always connect the two, but procrastination and perfectionism go hand in hand. Often when we push things off because the timing isn't right, it's because we want it to look like this perfect picture we have in our heads.

In an ideal world, my husband would take the kids somewhere all day. I would have tons of time to declutter and deep clean and be left with time to read a book and enjoy coffee. It would be glorious.

I was using the fact that that was pretty much never going to happen to allow me to push off my goal.

But what if instead of waiting to be able to do a single task for hours on end, we started to ask ourselves, "Can I focus for just fifteen minutes?"

In the next section of the book, we'll do a deep dive into the 15 Minute Formula for goal setting in particular, but right now, let's just start with changing our mindset.

In order to get more done of what matters, chip away at those goals, and get your time blocks and routines to stick. It's not about you being perfectly focused all day. It's about being focused in small chunks when you can. And sometimes, those single focused times happen inside your power pockets.

Using Power Pockets

Power pockets are a mom's secret weapon. If you went through the last chapter and created your ideal plans, you've got a pretty good feel for the potential of your schedule. And hopefully as you're continuing to read and finish the book, you'll start to implement your in-progress plans and see some immediate wins.

As you navigate this new schedule, you'll also start to see times where you can create power pockets. These are going to be times in your day where you can sneak in intentional tasks in fifteen minutes or less.

Once your schedule is going for about a week, create a list of these times. The key here is once you know when you have some power pockets, pre-identify what you're going to do during this time. You'll hear me say a lot that a big key to sticking with your routines and goals is being proactive vs. reactive.

See the thing is, time passes. We know this. Often, we get to the end of the day, toss our hands in the air, and wonder what we even did. But if we have a camera go back and watch us, we'd be able to find power pockets we could have used a little more strategically (and if you did your time inventory from Chapter 5, you'll know where they are too).

The Microwave Minute

The Microwave Minute is one of the easiest power pockets to use for intentional tasks. Technically, it's multitasking, but since we're focused and intentional about it, we're going to call it focused tasking.

How many times a day do you reheat that cup of coffee? Two? Maybe three? And what do you do while it's heating up? If you're like me and most of us, you're most likely grabbing your phone for a quick Facebook scroll, updating yourself on any emails that came in, or staring into space.

What if instead, we started to look at that time as an opportunity to get tasks done so they don't take up time later?

The concept is simple: every time you have something in the microwave, you're going to intentionally use that time to get done a tiny task. For me, it's emptying the dishwasher.

Now hear me out. I know that putting away two coffee mugs in the thirty seconds I'm at the microwave isn't going to change my life. But that time will add up, and throughout the day, you can get a ton done.

My suggestion to moms is always to make sure you load the dishes before bed. That way, during your microwave minutes, you can spend time unloading the dishwasher. After two to three times at the microwave, you'll have the entire thing unloaded, and it'll be ready to load up again. Instead of doing these tasks in one shot—which we can easily talk ourselves out of—being intentional about that time at the microwave allows us to get it off our list without even realizing it.

The key to using microwave minutes is the intentionality. As you can see below, I've got a list of some great microwave minute activities. If you go to www.the15minuteformula. com/free, you can print this list out in the 30-Day Action Guide and add it to your fridge. This way you'll always have something quick to refer to whenever your power pockets pop up—and you can suggest something to one of the kids as well.

microwave minute

FAST TASKS	GET ORGANIZED
✔ Put away dishes	✔ Create a task list
✔ Change over laundry	✔ Toss junk mail
✔ Wipe down counters	✔ Answer quick emails
✔ Load dishwasher	✔ Delete pictures on phone
✔ 15-minute pick-up	✔ Unsubscribe from emails
✔ Clear out fridge	✔ Plan some meals
✔ Sweep floor	✔ Update your budget

CAR LINE TASKS	QUICK TASKS
✔ Wipe down dashboard	✔ Quick pick-up
✔ Throw out junk	✔ Put away bags & shoes
✔ Text a friend	✔ Take out trash
✔ Listen to podcast	✔ Declutter one space
✔ Reading time	✔ Quick toilet clean
✔ Update to-do lists	✔ Read a devotional
✔ Make an appointment	✔ Write a Thank You note

Car Line Productivity

Another great time to use your microwave minutes or power pockets throughout the day is in the car. As moms, we often wear the hat of chauffeur. We can spend a lot of time in the car waiting at drop off or pick up, driving to and from activities, or just sitting.

So instead of just being in the car, why not use this as another intentional power pocket to work on some goals or get some tiny tasks done. Again, we've got to change our thoughts about these small times not being "enough" to really get things done. They will compound over time.

Back in Chapter 3, I talked about the compound effect and how fifteen minutes of time adds up, and it stands true here. Even five minutes in the car line each day equals twenty-five minutes a week. In twenty-five minutes, you can read a chapter of a book, make those phone calls needed, or clean out your car.

Let's ditch the all-or-nothing mentality here and realize that we can make huge gains in fifteen-minute chunks.

Again, your car line productivity is all about intentionality. Take some time to brainstorm out how much time you have in the car and what you'd like to do.

Now, when you have the minutes, you can choose to scroll social media or you can choose to chip away at some tiny tasks.

You could tell yourself that while you're waiting in the car line, you'll pull out a book or spend that time texting a friend each day to catch up. When you're shuffling kids to and from activities, you can determine that to be podcast time where you listen to some podcasts for your own growth (might I suggest downloading *The Purpose Driven Mom Show* wherever you podcast).

Now, instead of waiting for the perfect time, you can slowly use the compound effect to work on those micro priorities while you're waiting.

The Power of a Timer

Timers can be a mom's best friend.

There is something magical about a timer. It makes us all move a little faster, can gamify whatever we are doing, and gives us that urgency we need.

A great way to amplify your power pockets is to add in timers for urgency. If you're doing a fifteen-minute pick up in your home, dropping a timer will help you race against the clock. If you're looking to toss in some microwave minute tasks while dinner is on the stove, using a timer can help you feel urgency but not that you have to "do it all."

Timers are also great for your kids. Since my kids can't tell time, we don't use clock timers for them but songs. If we have some time before we have to go to karate, and I know my kids need to pick up their rooms today, I'll tell them that they have until two or three songs are finished to get things done. We'll push play on the Disney Hits station on Spotify (*The Greatest Showman* is another one of our favs) and get going.

The music makes the activity much more fun, and whatever doesn't get done by the end of the two songs can get done in the next power pocket. Even if you just play one song for pick up three to four times during the day, by the end of the day, the house will be in better shape, and then you and your family can spend the time after dinner hanging out together instead of mom nagging everyone to clean up before bed.

I also love to use podcasts as alternatives to timers. Instead of using my regular phone alarm, I'll tell myself that I'm going to sneak in a power pocket of picking up or folding laundry during this podcast. This is particularly motivating for me when it comes time to clean the shower—which is my least favorite of all the household tasks.

Tell yourself that you're going to listen to this twenty-minute episode, and your goal is to get your tiny task done before the episode is over. This way you've got a timer, you've got urgency, and you've got learning going on in your ear.

As a bonus, I suggest finding a podcast about the thing you want to do for extra motivation. For example, if I'm trying to sneak in decluttering to my power pocket, I might listen to the podcast called *A Slob Comes Clean* by Dana K. White where she talks all about decluttering. If my microwave minute task is balancing my bank account, I'll put on *Smart Money Mamas* by Chelsea Brennan. Or if I'm working on getting some tiny meal prep tasks in, I'll listen to an episode of *The Healthy Balanced Life* by Kristin Dovbniak to keep motivated. (And again, *The Purpose Driven Mom Show* is always a great one to use too! We do two episodes a week and our Monday episode if always fifteenish minutes, so it's perfect for a power pocket.)

Chapter 6 Action Steps

1. Head over to the Microwave Checklist in the Action Guide at www.the15minuteformula.com/free and pre-identify what items you'll do during your power pockets.
2. Find two to three podcasts to use as a timer during your tiny tasks.
3. Find a great channel on Spotify that your kids will love using as a timer alternative.

PILLAR #3

GOAL SETTING FOR BUSY MOMS

Chapter 7

Identify Your Goal and Vision

I love the new year. It's exciting. It's renewing. And it's when I get to use my brand-new planner.

And it used to be the time when I would put *way* too many things on my plate at once, get overwhelmed and mad at myself because I wasn't achieving what I thought I was supposed to, and quit by February.

According to a study in *Forbes* magazine, "Every year more than 50% of people make New Year's resolutions to lose weight, quit smoking, work out, save money, get a promotion, get a raise, and more. And yet, virtually every study tells us that around 80% of New Year's resolutions will get abandoned around this month. In fact, one study found that gym sales dropped precipitously from January to February."[3]

People aren't quitting their goals because they are lazy or awful or don't know how to achieve things. It's more likely because they created this super overwhelming plan that didn't make sense for their season.

We started this book talking all about the vision of the life you want to have. We do this because it's key to make sure we start with the end in mind. If you don't know where you want to go, what it will look or feel like, or those big plans for your future, you will struggle to create a plan that makes sense—and instead create a jam-packed plan that sets you up for failure.

The 15 Minute Formula has a lot of components you can use, but the quarterly planning system is its bread and butter. Without a seasonal goal-setting component, you won't know what to do in what order, and you'll struggle to gain traction.

Quarterly planning is perfect for you if you've been like me and continued to push your goals from year to year. I remember when it hit me that I needed to change the way I was setting goals.

I was decluttering my closet again (since it was a goal that I kept working on year after year and never seemed to gain any momentum with) and found a crumpled-up vision board from three years prior that I had made with some friends. I was excited to check it out and see how far I'd come on my goals.

My excitement pretty much crashed down when I noticed that the goals I had on that board were the same ones I had written down for that current year.

How was it three years later, and I was *still* trying to get it together?

I felt demoralized and like a failure. Three years had passed, and I felt like I hadn't done anything to progress my goals; I was stuck in the mud.

This is when I knew something had to change.

Someone recommended the book *The 12 Week Year* by Brian P. Moran, and it made lightbulbs go off inside my head. The concept was simple enough—stop planning year by year and plan quarter by quarter. This simple concept got my wheels spinning until I came up with the 15 Minute Formula. Because while the principles in it are amazing, they just don't always make sense for a busy mom.

Before we jump into how you are going to apply this as a busy mom, let's break down the basics.

When we make our goals year to year, we are giving ourselves *too* much space and not enough urgency.

Maybe you make a plan to read twenty-five books in a year—great goal! But you pretty much forget about it for a while, and then in October, you remember that you wanted to read all those books. Now, instead of having all twelve months to work on your goal, you're left with three. And to read twenty-five books in just three months is super daunting, so you decide to quit and try again next year.

Perhaps your goal was to create a sinking fund (where you save all year for things) for the holidays so you have

$1,000 put aside by November. You do great in January and add your monthly $100 to your envelope. But in February, you spend the money somewhere else, and by March you've forgotten about it completely. Now when the holiday comes around, you've got nothing saved and need to put it all on your credit cards. Now you feel pretty bad about that goal you set for yourself.

These things happen because you are giving yourself too much freedom and time to complete things. Instead of looking at your goals as something you want to accomplish by the end of the calendar year, let's create a quarterly plan and vision.

Starting with the Yearly Goals

Before we jump in, I want you to change your mindset around having to do things aligned with the calendar. Listen, I get it—the calendar is great and refreshing and gives us some deadlines, but it's just a calendar.

From now on, when I talk about your year or your quarter, know that I am not talking about how it lines up with the seasons or the calendar. I'm talking about the next twelve months for *you* and the next twelve weeks for *you*. If they line up with the calendar, that's awesome. And if they don't, that's okay too.

Too often, we get so caught up with what the calendar says that if we don't have our goals or plans together before January 1 or even Monday, we'll keep pushing things off until the next week, month, or year. You have the power to start your year or quarter whenever you want. Please stop waiting for Monday or the first—empower yourself to start now.

If we are going to use this quarterly goal-setting module, I do want you to think of the next calendar year and the goals you want to achieve. While we aren't going to create our initial plans around what you want to achieve in an entire year (remember, we need more urgency built in), this will allow us to map out your themes for the quarters and make a plan that builds on itself.

Looking at the next twelve months, I want you to complete a brain dump of all the things you want to accomplish. In the next chapter we'll talk about three types of goals and how to make an action plan around them. So for now, grab a piece of paper (or better yet head to www.the15minuteformula.com/free and download the free 30-Day Action Guide workbook) and start to brain dump.

Put on a fifteen-minute timer (you know we love those over here!) and jot down all the things you want to accomplish. The sky's the limit! For this first time through, don't put a filter on your dreams. Don't worry if they don't make sense or how you'll accomplish them.

I want you to get them from your head onto the paper. We'll talk about a filtering process soon, but I think it's so important to allow yourself time and space to dream and think about your goals. This is a great activity to do with your partner or kids as well. Put on some music and a timer and just ask them to create their list (and if they are little, you can make it for them). So often as busy moms we don't give ourselves any space to dream. I encourage you to make this a routine you do each quarter.

By getting all of these exciting things from your brain onto the page, you'll start to get an idea of the direction you want things to go. This will help you create your vision—and immediately start to see some outliers.

Starting to Categorize

After you've done your dream big brain dump, now we'll start to filter and organize your goals into categories. These categories are going to help you see which goals go together, which fit a common theme, and which ones stand out on their own.

I suggest folding your paper into three or four sections (or more if you need—and again, we have this done for you in the Action Guide) and rewriting those goals into common categories or areas.

For example, you might have that you want to go on a family vacation, pay off a credit card, or start a business. These could all fall under the financial category.

You might also want to work on your morning routine, read thirty books, and meet up with your friends once a month for coffee. These could all go under the personal category.

I suggest rewriting these goals instead of just highlighting or coding them on the current list you've made. When we write our goals and dreams out, we can affirm what we want to achieve in our brain and help enroll our brains in this vision as well! This is key when your limiting beliefs and brain will want to work against some of your goals (but more on that in my next book).

Remember not to cross things off or filter them if they feel too big for you or you don't think they make sense right now—we're not at that stage! Just place them with similar goals and then create a list of goals that don't seem to fit with any categories and are off to the side by themselves.

Creating Themes for Your Quarterly Goals

Now that we've got your big dreams and goals for the next twelve months out on paper and categorized, it's time to put on the filters and determine what makes sense to go where.

I am going to encourage you *not* to work on all of your goals at the same time. Actually, I think the fewer goals you are focusing on the better.

When you focus on fewer goals, you can grow confidence, consistency, and depth instead of being scattered and all over the place.

Now hear me out. I am not saying that you shouldn't go after every single goal you want to achieve in the next twelve months. I am suggesting that you are strategic about *when* you work on them. This isn't about not dreaming big or cutting your potential short. When you use the 15 Minute Formula quarterly goal process, you're saying, "this doesn't make the most sense at this moment, and instead, I will work on it later." And I want you to actually pick when later is—because if we don't pick the date, it won't happen.

So how do you figure out what to work on when?

Let's refer back to Chapters 1 and 2 (and hopefully you completed the action items from those chapters so you're ready to jump in) where we talked about making your vision and seasonal priorities.

In chapter 1, I mentioned four seasons you should add into your year.

A season of rest and fun

A season of productivity

A season of busy

A season of planning

Keep these seasons in mind as we plan out what you'll be working on each quarter. Remember that each season doesn't have to be an entire twelve weeks or even an entire month and that you have the power to customize things! Make sure you're adding these into your quarterly plans so you don't burn out and actually enjoy working on goals instead of just being a goal chaser!

A Little Bit about Being a Goal Chaser

Whew. I've been here before.

I make a goal. I make a plan. I achieve a goal. I work on the next goal. Rinse and repeat.

Have you been there too?

Where you don't leave any time for celebration? Where you head from goal to goal? Where you get tunnel vision on achievement and don't enjoy the process and journey at all?

As we get deep into goal setting, I want you to identify if you find yourself goal chasing and making sure you take time to pause and reflect on how much you have accomplished—no matter how big or small.

I know that we feel like we have a million things to accomplish and do, but if you're always just looking toward the finish line—the fully decluttered house, the business you start, the 5k you train for—you'll miss all the incredible moments along the way.

I remember running my first 5k and how hard it felt at the time. I used to use mailboxes to measure my distance.

I would celebrate every dang mailbox I passed each run. This allowed me to celebrate myself along the way too. I wasn't going to win the race or get a personal record—I simply wanted to complete it. And if the actual race was all I celebrated, I would have felt a bit of a letdown when it was over.

Remember, showing up for your goals in any way is something to celebrate. Let's say goodbye to hustle and achieving for achievement's sake and lean into your power and consistency.

Before we pick which goals go where, we need to lay out the next twelve months to see what makes the most sense. You don't want to put a million goals in a quarter where you have a vacation or a heavy work project—that is just a recipe for disaster and burnout!

First, list out the next twelve months and any big events happening or refer back to the list you made in Chapter 2. This is going to help you decide which goals make sense where.

Let's work through an example!

Month	Event
January	Nothing Really!
February	Lots of Family Birthdays
March	Family Vacation
April	Big Yearly Work Event

May	Nothing Really!
June	End of School Year Activities
July	Kids Home for Summer
August	Family Vacation
September	Back to School
October	Fall Sports Start
November	Holidays
December	Holidays

Don't get too bogged down in the specifics of exactly what is happening and the dates, just make sure you have an overview of what is happening for your family. As you can see in this example, January and May are lighter months with nothing really on our plates. What this tells me is that those are great months to go heavier with some of my goals because I'll have more time to focus on them.

So how do you plan the other months?

I want you to start to create themes for each month around what makes sense for the events you have going on that month *or* in the future.

For example, if you know that you are going to be hosting for the holidays and having lots of people over during the course of November and December, you might want to create a decluttering or deep cleaning goal for October. This way, you're working on what needs to be done *before* it needs to

119

be done—instead of scrambling to do it then!

Let's go back to our examples and create themes for our goals based on events happening that month or in the next few months.

Month	Event	Theme
January	Nothing Really!	Personal Goals
February	Lots of Family Birthdays	Family Time
March	Family Vacation	Cleaning Routines
April	Big Yearly Work Event	Self-Care Goals
May	Nothing Really!	Personal Goals
June	End of School Year Activities	Budgeting and Finances
July	Kids Home for Summer	Family Time
August	Family Vacation	Morning Routines
September	Back to School	Meal Planning
October	Fall Sports Start	Decluttering
November	Holidays	Deep Cleaning
December	Holidays	Goal Setting for Next Year

As you can see, I was super strategic about my themes for each month. If I know that April contains a big work project, I am going to have to be intentional about self-care and make sure that's a priority. If I know that the summer means vacation and kids home, the month before would be a great time to work on our budgeting so that we're able to have fun with less stress. Since October might be a little crazy with all the sports starting, it makes sense to work on meal planning in September and get a ton of freezer meals stocked.

There will be other goals that you work on that aren't 100% aligned with your monthly theme (these are called numerical goals, and we'll break those down in the next chapter), and that's okay. You'll also have some goals that are routine based that you carry on from month to month— awesome! I'm not saying that you stop working on those just because they don't fit your theme.

By having predetermined themes, you're focusing on a specific area and know exactly where you can put your other goals. Remember, it's not saying that you're never working on them, it's saying you're working on them when they make the most sense.

Now that you have your themes set up, refer back to the categorized goal sheet you completed. It's time to plop these goals into the appropriate month and add some order to them. I don't want to give you a hard and fast rule of how many goals you should work on each month but as a guideline, I'd suggest picking around three per theme as your focus (and remember, you'll have some goals cross over from the previous month, and we can work on them in parallel).

For each month, I suggest you pick

1 project-based goal (think of these as goals that have multiple tasks to complete)

1 routine-based goal

1 learning goal

We'll go into more detail in the next chapter on these types of goals.

Let's do an example for April when the theme is self-care.

My project-based goal might be working on knitting a blanket or creating a scrapbook for my family (if these are things I enjoy doing).

My routine could be adding in a five-minute meditation before I go to bed to unwind.

My learning could be reading a book on self-care or listening to podcasts for my mindset each day during my drive into work.

Make sure when you complete your plan, you refer back to the goals you originally set for yourself to see where they fit in. If you find that you have two project goals and only one month planned for that theme, you might want to work on that theme two times a year. In my example, each month had a different theme, but there is nothing wrong with having themes fall over the course of a few months or touching on a theme again later in the year. It's all up to you, your season, and what fits your priority-based productivity during this twelve-month span of time.

And don't forget, just because my example was based on the calendar year doesn't mean your quarters need to align. We're using a model where you're going to figure out what makes sense for you twelve weeks at a time. Instead of saying, "This is what I will accomplish at the end of the year," we'll be saying, "This is what I will accomplish at the end of these twelve weeks."

By giving yourself more urgency, you're more likely to stick to your goals and achieve them faster. Parkinson's Law proves this: the amount of work required adjusts to the time available to complete. If you say you're going to complete something by the end of the year, it'll take you the entire year (or more). But if you say you'll complete it by the end of the twelve weeks, you're more likely to complete it by the end of the twelve weeks.

Now that we've created your themes for your goals and started to plan out when you'll work on what, it's time to tackle how to break these goals down and create an action plan for them. We're going to do that in the next chapter, so before you turn the page, make sure you do this part!

Chapter 7 Action Steps

1. Write down your big events for the next few months.
2. Plan your themes for each month based on the events.
3. Do your best to jot down a learning, project, and routine goal that fit the themes based on your twelve-month vision (and head to www.the15minuteformula.com/free to get the workbook to make it easier).

A Quick Note to You: The 3 Types of Goals

Your goals should not be one-size-fits-all, but for some reason, we struggle to look at them any differently.

I've been creating goals forever. Even as a little kid, I was making goals and working toward them. Whether it was a badge I wanted to get when I was in Girl Scouts, money I wanted to save at my part-time job, or honor roll in high school—I was all about goals.

Napoleon Hill says it best: "A goal is a dream with a deadline," and we know that if we don't craft a goal around something that we dream of doing, it's far less likely that we actually achieve it.

But there is more to goal setting than just writing down what you want. In the previous chapter, I asked you to go through and brain dump all your dreams onto paper and categorize them into themes. (You did that, right?)

Now that you've got all your big dreams for the next twelve months written down and you've picked your themes for the next twelve weeks, let's look at the types of goals you might have so you can make sure your goals are well rounded. I'll also talk about specific ways to break each of them down.

Chapter 8

Numerical Goals

Numerical goals are my favorite type of goals to start with when it comes to action planning because I find that they are the easiest to break down. They also are the goals that we can take the emotion out of and just look at the data. I'm a huge data nerd, and I think that we get way too emotional about our goals. You're going to hear me reference the phrase "data over drama" a lot throughout the rest of *The 15 Minute Formula,* and it's because we need to stop getting caught up in the emotions of goals and really look at our actual progress.

Numerical goals are simply goals that can easily be broken down by numbers and math. These are often goals that span over the course of the entire year, and that's why it's key to know your vision for your next twelve months so you can start working on them now.

Here are some examples of numerical goals:

- I want to run 50 miles this year.
- I want to read 24 books this year.
- I want to save $10,000 this year.

When it comes to goal planning, I suggest you always start with these goals because, like I mentioned, they will span over the course of the year, and you'll want to make sure you break them down for all twelve months and then your specific quarter.

Let's break down a reading goal together when it comes to quarterly planning!

If you say you want to read twenty-four books in the year, simply divide twenty-four by four (quarters in your year—remember, it doesn't have to perfectly match up with the calendar year, just twelve-week chunks).

Now I'm left with six books in a quarter. Well, I know that there are three months per quarter, so I'll divide that six by three which leads me to reading two books per month.

Whew, okay—that feels much more doable than reading twenty-four books during the entire year. Now that you know the numerical goal you're shooting for each month, it's time to take it a step further.

If I know that I want to read two books per month, I am going to look at my themes for the next twelve weeks and ask myself if there are any books I want to read that support those themes. For example, if I know one month has a decluttering focus, I might want to read *Decluttering at the Speed of Life* by Dana K. White. If a month has a morning routine focus, I might add to my list to read the *Miracle Morning* by Hal Elrod.

After I've planned which books I am going to read during that quarter, I can now see how many books I still need to pick to read.

If you have a similar goal, I want to encourage you to pick the books you plan to read *before* your twelve weeks starts. This way you know exactly what the plan is and won't waste time getting the book from the library, trying to figure out what to read next, or getting off track when you lose momentum.

Now that you've got the books planned, let's keep going! The thing about the 15 Minute Formula goal-setting framework is that we want to make your plan as overwhelm-proof as possible.

I know it doesn't always seem fun to sit and break down goals when you have a ton of other things on your plate, but trust me that if you spend the time *before* the quarter or the month doing this work, you'll achieve more because you know where to get started on things and you start the month feeling ahead of the game with an empowered plan.

As we continue with our reading example, the next step in breaking down a numerical goal is to find out how many pages are in each of the books you want to read (a quick Google search can tell you if you don't have the book yet) and divide up those pages by the number of days in a month that you plan to read.

I never actually suggest that anyone plans to do anything for seven days a week. It's a setup for failure. I think five days a week is enough to work on your goals and create a new habit over time while giving you buffer time for when life throws you off. Because we know it will! This way, if you've got five days a week planned out, and something comes up and you don't work on your goals that day, you still have two days of wiggle room! And guess what? If you do work on it seven days a week, way to go! You've done a bonus and gotten ahead, which gives you more wiggle room for the future when something else might pop up!

If a book has 250 pages and I plan on reading twenty-five days in the month, I know that I just need to read ten pages a day to complete it by the end of the month.

Ten pages. That's it.

Ten pages is doable. Ten pages can be done in just fifteen minutes. Ten pages can be done in between opening the Play-Doh containers or breaking up sibling fights. Ten pages is a lot more manageable than the big numerical goal of "I am going to read twenty-four books."

Once you've got that broken down and know how many pages to read each day, it's time to assign them to days. The way that I suggest you do this is not by planning the specific day for each ten-page section but by assigning the weeks beforehand.

Check out the example below to see what I mean!

So, if I was to breakdown a 220-page book before the quarter began, my chart or breakdown would look like this:

Week 1	Week 2	Week 3	Week 4
Pages 1–10	Pages 55–65	Pages 110–120	Pages 165–175
Pages 11–21	Pages 66–76	Pages 121–131	Pages 176–186
Pages 22–32	Pages 77–87	Pages 132–142	Pages 187–197
Pages 33–43	Pages 88–98	Pages 143–153	Pages 198–208
Pages 44–54	Pages 99–109	Pages 154–164	Pages 209–220

Before the quarter starts, I now know exactly which pages or chapters need to get done beforehand. This gives me that self-created urgency we talked about when it comes to quarterly planning. Now in the back of our mind, we know that if we take too many days off, we'll start to get off track.

Each week now when you start your weekly planning (which we talk about in Chapter 14), you'll reference your original chart and *then* you'll assign which days to work on this specific goal. The reason we don't plan the week out that far in advance is because life is *going* to happen. You may want to read every Tuesday, but what if a school event pops up on a Tuesday? It doesn't make sense to try to cram it in or stay up late or get stressed about the fact that you must read on Tuesday. You have flexibility to move the day around based on what the week needs. This is another reason why we only break our goals down for five days in the week—allowing space and margin for life to happen!

When you look at your goals, make sure you create multiple numerical goals to work on throughout the year or the quarter and continue to check in and adjust them as you go.

If your numerical goal was to save $10,000 in a year and one month you were unable to save anything, before the next month begins, you'll go in and audit and readjust that goal and those numbers to help you stay on track. This helps things not spring up on you ("Oh man, I forgot about this savings goal, and now I need to save $10,000 in a month to hit it! Guess I'll just quit!) and allows you to adjust as needed. There might even be months where you get ahead on your goal and can adjust to have less on your plate!

Chapter 8 Action Steps

1. Using your themes, determine your numerical goals for the next twelve weeks.
2. Break them down using the formula so you can add them to your plan.

Chapter 9

Project-Based Goals

While numerical goals tend to be ones that span over the course of your twelve months, I suggest you create a project-based goal each month to fit your theme and give you urgency. When we have these bigger project-based goals and try to make them happen by the end of the year, we tend to procrastinate because we are overwhelmed with where to start.

So, what is a project-based goal?

I consider a project-based goal anything that can't be broken down numerically and instead must be broken down by task.

One of the most common project-based goals that the moms in my community work on would be decluttering. Decluttering your house tends to be something that goes on people's lists and never gets completed because they feel like it's too big of a project to start.

Here are some other examples of project-based goals:

- making a scrapbook for your child's first year
- planning a birthday party or bridal shower
- organizing a section of your home
- getting an event together for work
- completing a quilting project

As you can see, these goals aren't as cut and dry as the numerical goals, and therefore, simple math won't help you break them down, just yet. They also aren't goals you want to drag out, so again remember, I suggest you work on *one* project-based goal for a month or quarter.

Step 1: Break Down a Project-Based Goal

Whereas numerical goals rely on math to break them down, here we're going to rely on *tasks* and *time*.

Project-based goals are the things that moms struggle with the most. When you already have so much on your plate and you're pretty exhausted, it can feel hard to figure out how to work on your goals.

So instead of looking at the big project and just assuming you'll start "when you're motivated," let's make a strategic plan that will have you moving toward your goals fifteen minutes at a time.

I know I've said it before in the book, but I just want to remind you of the power of fifteen minutes. Fifteen minutes can fly by in an instant scrolling on my phone. But fifteen minutes added up over the course of a month or a quarter can allow you to complete your project. We need to stop looking at fifteen minutes as not enough and realize that any time spent on your goals is better than no time spent on your goals—and that fifteen minutes a day is *amazing!*

When breaking down a project-based goal, you're going to start by listing out all of the tasks you need to do to complete the project and categorizing them. This will allow you to create an order that makes sense.

Let's look at the decluttering example and how we could break it down into small chunks.

I would start with listing every room that I wanted to declutter and list them on my paper.

Kitchen   **Bedroom**   **Playroom**

As you can see, I've started with listing three rooms in my house. By starting with the rooms, I can now focus my list on each room. After I've got the rooms listed, I'm going to put on a fifteen-minute timer and jot down everything that must be decluttered in each room by section or what I think would take me approximately fifteen minutes (or less). By the end of the fifteen minutes, my list might look like this:

Kitchen	Bedroom	Playroom
Spices	Top of Dresser	Legos
Tupperware	Coats	Dolls
Pots and Pans	Dresser Drawer #1	Cars
Silverware	Dresser Drawer #2	Books
Kitchen Gadgets	Dresser Drawer #3	Puzzles
Fridge	Closet—Shirts	Play-Doh
Freezer	Closet—Pants	Stuffed Animals
Pantry	Closet—Sweaters	Trains
Top of Fridge	Purses	Arts and Crafts #1
Outside of Fridge	Belts	Arts and Crafts #2

As you can see, in the kitchen I simply separated it by area and item because that made the most sense and I knew I could do one section in fifteen minutes. In the bedroom and playroom, there were a few bigger areas, and I knew that my closet or dresser was too big of a project to finish in just fifteen minutes, so I split it up. If you have bigger areas like this, you can break them into multiple fifteen-minute chunks to work on throughout the week.

With project-based goals, your job is to create these fifteen-minute breakdowns *before* you ever begin the project so that you know exactly what to work on and when. We often don't want to take the time to complete these breakdowns because of the time they will take, but we will waste a ton of time figuring out where to pick up on a project or procrastinating because we're overwhelmed with the task in front of us. By having these fifteen-minute chunks predetermined (and then adding them into your weekly plan that we'll talk about soon), you'll be able to just get started. If you complete your fifteen-minute task for the day and want to be done, great job! Pat yourself on the back and keep going. If you feel inspired to keep working, that's amazing! Now you can get ahead and start to build in more buffer time for yourself!

Let's look at another example. Say you want to create a scrapbook for your child's first year. There are lots of steps involved, but once you break it down, the project will be more doable and fit better into your schedule. Again the goal is just fifteen minutes, five times a week to work on it!

First, let's categorize!

Organize	Buy	Decorate
Culling Phone Photos #1	Order Prints from Website	Organize Printed Pictures #1
Culling Phone Photos #2	Order Scrapbook	Organize Printed Pictures #2
Culling Phone Photos #3	Buy Any Stickers	Organize Printed Pictures #3

Culling Phone Pictures #4	Buy Cutting Tools	Organize Printed Photos #4
Organize Any Photos	Research Other Ideas	Organize Printed Printed Pictures#5
Search Facebook Page #1		Complete Month #1
Search Facebook Page #2		Complete Month #2

As you can see for this project, I started to break tasks down and made sure that anything that would take more than fifteen minutes was chunked out into multiple sessions. I know that going through and culling (doing some fast deletes of pictures I want to delete) is going to take a while since I have over 4,000 phone photos. Instead of just making it a huge task to do and then getting overwhelmed while thinking about how many pictures I have to go through, I am going to separate it into multiple fifteen-minute sessions. This way I know that over the course of four sessions, I am going to put on a fifteen-minute timer and do what I can. When the timer goes off, I'll either pat myself on the back for doing a good job and hitting my time or keep going!

Step 2: Turn Your Project-Based Goal Into a Numerical Goal

Once you've got your goal broken down, it now turns into a numerical goal, and we can rely back on math to create your plan! When you start to implement the 15 Minute Formula into your goals, productivity, and day, you'll start to see there is so much overlap in the systems. And since we know that numerical goals are the easiest to break down, let's decrease our overwhelm with your goal even more and break it down with some simple math!

Before we start, we need to know if your project-based goal is one that you want to complete at the end of the month (maybe it aligns with your theme) or at the end of your quarter. This is going to completely depend on how big of a goal it is. Don't worry if something fits your theme for month one but not for month two—let it overlap! As a busy mom, it doesn't make sense to just rush things to get them done. Give yourself the urgency and a deadline, but remember to make it realistic for your season!

For example, if I were to break down the decluttering goal, I would first ask myself if it would make sense for me to complete this goal over the course of a month or a twelve-week period. If the goal is too big to complete in fifteen-minute tasks in one month, I would have it span over my quarter. I know that decluttering my home would definitely not get done in fifteen-minute chunks in just one month! I could potentially get one or two rooms done a month, but that's it. And if I tried to jam it in, I would be setting myself up for failure and frustration and just burnout and quit. Therefore, I know that a decluttering goal is better suited to be a twelve-week goal.

If I looked at organizing my scrapbook, I would see that while I have a lot of tasks on my plate, it is perhaps doable to complete in four to six weeks. Instead of having this goal span the course of the entire quarter, I may make a goal to complete it sooner.

Once you know how long you want to give yourself to complete the goal, give it a due date. Yup, write that due date in your planner and commit to it. This could be four weeks, six weeks, or the entire twelve weeks of your quarter.

Now let's do some math. If I know that I want to declutter my house by the end of twelve weeks, it's time to determine how many tasks I have to complete each week (or even each day) to hit my deadline.

For easy math, let's pretend that after my brain dump and categorization, I found that I have twelve sections/rooms in my house. Perfect! Now I know that I need to complete one room per week in order to hit my goal by the end of the twelve weeks (12 weeks / 12 rooms = 1 room a week).

To take it a step further, *before* your quarter starts, I

want you to figure out how many tasks you need to complete each day. You won't pre-assign them to dates yet, but it's key to know how many days a week you might have to work on something.

Because here is the thing: I am going to suggest you work on your goals in fifteen-minute chunks throughout the week. But depending on the amount of tasks needed to complete your goal, this might be one 15-minute chunk a day or two 15-minute chunks a day. So, let's do the math.

If I see that my kitchen has ten sections to it and I know I want to work on my goal five days a week, simple math can let me know how many fifteen-minute chunks I need to complete: 10 sections / 5 days = two 15-minute chunks a day.

Awesome! I now have my plan mapped out and know that for the "kitchen week," I only need to create two 15-minute chunks five days a week, and the entire kitchen can be done by the end of the week. Since I determined that I need to complete one room a week to complete this goal in twelve weeks, I would need to go ahead and figure out how many fifteen-minute chunks I need each week for each specific room. I'd suggest you then map it out in advance so that you can see the vision and the big picture—this will help with procrastination. Since you know that if you get off track, you're throwing the entire plan off, it will most likely be easier to convince yourself to just put on your timer and work on your goal for fifteen minutes than not!

Chapter 9 Action Steps

1. Using your themes, determine your project-based goals for your twelve weeks.
2. Break down those projects using the 15 Minute Formula.
3. Check out the action guide at www.the15minuteformula.com/free for some more examples.

Chapter 10

Routine and Habit-Based Goals

This third type of goal is my favorite to talk about: routine and habit-based goals. All goals will have routines and habits inside of them. You might start with a project-based goal, use the numerical goal system to get specific on when you're doing what, and then still need to use this formula to make the routine or habit stick—it's just so cool to see how connected it all is.

I used to struggle with keeping my habits for the long term. I can't even tell you how many times I tried to start a great morning routine before making it midweek and quitting. My health goals were even worse—I've been on this journey to love and embrace my body while making it healthy since I was ten years old.

Before I had my kids, I had lost seventy pounds and was super proud of myself, but it came at a cost. In order to lose the seventy pounds, I began to feel obsessive about my exercise and would jog close to five miles a day *and* make it to the gym. I obsessed over everything I ate and tried to feed myself the fewest calories possible, not caring at all about ingredients or actual health (hello, sugar-free Jell-O and every other thing that '90s diet culture told us was good for us).

When I had my kids, I figured I would just do the exact same things to lose the baby weight—but my body completely rebelled. I was sleep deprived, breastfeeding, and a hormonal mess, and those same all-or-nothing tactics were not going to fit into my schedule and my life. But I kept trying.

I would start the same diet over and over again, be so overwhelmed with the restrictions, quit by Wednesday, and vow to start again Monday.

You remember that Monday Mentality we talked about earlier, right? Here I was trying to do it all over again.

Eventually, I got tired of the yo-yo with my health and wanted to try something different. Instead of doing everything, getting overwhelmed, quitting within a few days, and then berating and shaming myself for being awful (you've been there, right?), I thought, *What if I just slowed down? What if I just worked on my health in tiny chunks and was proud of what I accomplished instead of focusing on where I struggled?*

Hence the concept of routine stacking was born.

I had finally come up with a way to ditch my perfectionism and all-or-nothing mentality and actually start to see success with small changes.

Using Routine Stacking for Your Goals

For any routine or habit-based goal you have, using routine stacking will allow you to see success and make changes that actually stick.

There are a few steps to getting it done:

- Map out the vision for your routine.
- Use the numerical goal system to determine how long you want to work on each stage.
- Utilize the track and stack method to grow at a pace that makes sense for you.

The concept of routine stacking is simple—instead of trying to do it all, I want you to pick one to two habits each week (or longer) to stick with, and then grow it when you're ready. Now you're going to grow your confidence that you are capable of creating this new routine while also making the routine stick!

I've used this same concept when I wanted to get up earlier. Have you been there? You know you want to get up earlier. I mean, everyone says you *have* to get up at 5 a.m., right? So, you decide you'll start Monday. Monday is great:

you bound out of bed and feel energized. But the shock is too much to your body that is used to getting up at 7 a.m., so by Tuesday, that snooze button looks too good to not tap and your body rebels to get more sleep.

What if you routine stacked it?

Instead of starting at 5 a.m., just get up fifteen minutes earlier. On Monday you get up at 6:45. It may not feel like a huge difference, but it's a slow wake-up for your body, and honestly, it's just fifteen minutes—you can convince your brain of that. You wake up at 6:45 for a few days or even a week and then you add fifteen minutes. Now you're up at 6:30, and it doesn't feel like as much of a shock. Slowly you move that wake-up time by fifteen minutes, and a month or so later, you're hitting your wake-up goal, and it doesn't even feel that hard (most days).

This is the power of using routine stacking.

Step 1: Mapping Out the Vision for Your Routine

Here I go again—but we've got to start with the end in mind. By knowing where you want to go, you can craft your routines and work toward them with focus.

Before you jump into any routine—whether it's health, self-care, or your morning routine—don't skip this step!

Refer back to the time blocks we created in Chapter 4 and jot down between four and twelve things you'd like to see inside that routine or time block.

Let's use an evening routine example to really break this down.

If I could dream of my ideal evening routine (let's say this block goes from 7 p.m.–11 p.m. and my theme is home/ personal), I might make a list that looks like this:

Ideal Evening Routine:

- Load dishwasher
- Make lunches for tomorrow
- Clean counter spaces
- Refer to planner for tomorrow and check in with today's goals
- Wash my face
- Watch a show with Hubby
- 5-minute meditation to unwind
- Read book

Now before I started routine stacking, I would look at this list and decide on Monday I was going to do all of these things. By Tuesday night, I'd be tired and not want to do anything and quit by Wednesday telling myself if I wasn't so lazy I'd actually get things done.

Sound familiar?

Instead let's use routine stacking to create an evening routine you can stick with.

But, Cara, won't it take forever to get the routine down?

No. Not forever—but definitely longer than doing it all at once.

Can I ask you a question? Has that worked for you yet? That thing where you overwhelm yourself and put too much on your plate and then quit?

What if instead, you gave yourself space and time to make things stick, allowing yourself to not go at a rapid pace and instead add things to the routine 5–15 minutes at a time?

So now, let's move to the next step: creating a numerical-based plan for your routines.

Step 2: Using the Numerical Goal Formula to Make Your Plan

Oh look, numerical goals, we meet again!

There is a reason I teach numerical goal breakdowns first. It's because everything always leads back to them! And when we can take the emotions out and just look at the math of your goal, you can make a plan that makes sense for you and your season.

So how can we use the numerical goal concept with our evening routine stack?

The first question you need to ask yourself is "Realistically, when would I like this routine to be solid?"

Once you know how long you want to take to work on it, we can do the math.

For our evening routine example, let's say that I want to have this routine done in two months. Since I have eight tasks listed, my math is easy!

8 weeks / 8 tasks = 1 task per week

You might break it down to work on two tasks each week or add in a new part of the routine every three days or stick to one task for two weeks—it's completely up to you!

Once the math is done and I know how many tasks I need each week, it's time to plan so that I know what I will work on when—starting with just *one* task and adding another each week.

Here's an evening routine breakdown:

evening routine

TASK	WEEK 1	WEEK 2	WEEK 3	WEEK 4	WEEK 5	WEEK 6	WEEK 7	WEEK 8
Load dishes		■	■	■	■	■	■	■
Make lunches			■	■	■	■	■	■
Counters & trash				■	■	■	■	■
Quick pick-up					■	■	■	■
Fast sweep						■	■	■
Nightly reflection							■	■
Tomorrow's plan								■
PM meditation								

See how slowly adding in things each week increases the time my routine takes without getting super overwhelmed by everything I have to do?

And the best part? Using this formula, you'll most likely have days where you do more than you planned—which is a huge confidence boost!

Since you know the vision for your ideal routine, something like this might happen . . .

It's day one and you load the dishwasher in less than ten minutes. You stop and say, "that's it?" and realize it didn't take as long as you thought.

Now you have two options: pat yourself on the back and say good job for achieving your goal of the day and go do something else, or you can get ahead. Since you know that next week making lunches is on the list, you figure why not? Might as well do this tonight since I feel like it.

You feel great for doing some bonus work and mentally start to realize it's possible to add these things into your evening without them taking a ton of time.

And if the next day you get done with the dishwasher but don't feel like doing anything else? Awesome—that was just a bonus anyway, and you'll get to it consistently next week!

Slowly over time, you'll continue to add things in, grow your confidence that you're able to get this done, and ditch the overwhelm that comes with doing it all at once.

Step 3: Utilize the Track and Stack Method to Grow at a Pace that Makes Sense for You

Completing your routines feels great, but by using the track and stack method, you're able to see when and how you should grow. There are going to be weeks where you won't accomplish and hit your goals and routine stacks—it's inevitable.

So how do you know when it's time to add a new task or when you should repeat the week to improve?

First, you need to be tracking.

I use a program called Trello to track things online (make sure you go to www.the15minuteformula.com/free where I have a free Trello tracking board for you), but you can use a notepad, to-do list, habit app, or anything you want!

Make sure each night or the next morning you track whether you hit your routine or not. A simple check mark is not only satisfying (tell me I'm not the only one who writes things down to cross them out), but also lets you know how you can continue to grow this goal.

Remember, I don't actually suggest making a goal to complete something for seven days. None of us are perfect, and by shooting for seven days, you're setting yourself up for failure and not leaving a buffer for life to happen.

But what about consistency, you might ask?

I get it, there are tons of productivity experts talking about twenty-one days in a row and how you have to do something every day for it to be a habit, but I wonder how many of them are moms. How many of them try to be consistent but have a teething baby up all night so need that extra fifteen minutes of a snooze? How many of them want to make sure they get their dishwasher loaded each night but need to stay up late helping the teen with homework?

Five days is great, it's enough, and it leads with grace—which we need as moms.

My suggestion is to aim to complete something for at least five days, but you can start with three if you want to—it all depends on your personal starting point. I also suggest you come up with a goal minimum. While completing something 100% of the days is amazing, I think anything 80% or higher is great!

Let's head back to our evening routine.

My week one goal is to load the dishwasher for five days in a row, and I hit it! Since I hit my goal, I'm ready to stack a new task.

Week two comes and I hit my dishwasher goal for four out of five days (woohoo!), but only made lunches two out of five days.

I suggest you repeat this stack to get more consistency while adjusting your goals.

In week three, my goal is to load the dishwasher five out of five days and make lunches three out of five days. See how I didn't go back to the five out of five that I originally planned but instead just inched this goal a tiny bit. At the end of this week ,if I've hit my dishwasher goal and my lunch goal (remember just three out of five days now), I'd feel confident stacking a new piece of the routine.

So as I go into week four, I've got a dishwasher to load (five out of five days), lunches I want to make (four out of five days—see how we increased again), and I am going to aim for five out of five days cleaning and wiping down the counters.

While it sets your plan off track a week, you've done more for yourself by not quitting and creating a more realistic goal to work toward. I see a lot of people who would use this concept but not add anything else to their stack until they hit their metrics 100%—they either do it five out of five days or they have to start over.

Then they are stuck on the routine hamster wheel over and over again instead of growing it slowly; no matter what the number, they get stuck on loading their dishwasher for months because they didn't do it perfectly.

Let's change the way we look at progress—it's not about perfection. It's about intention. And by showing up in small and steady increments for your goals, you'll gain more progress and achieve more than when you had to do things all in or perfectly.

Routine stacking is also amazing for you and your kids. One of my clients Kim C. used this concept with her kids when they were just three and five years old. She knew they needed to create a routine for flossing their teeth, but it wasn't something that was consistent in her home.

Since flossing was a habit she struggled with too, she broke down the routine to help her kids make it a habit that sticks. They started with just flossing every other day, and she would reward them on a chart to track their progress and celebrate.

After a few weeks, she noticed her kids were asking her to floss more! They would ask if it was a floss day or not and wanted to do it. This let her know that it was time to add on. They had finally made flossing consistent!

Now her kids flossing is just something that happens in their day, and since she started a good habit like this so early for them, I doubt they'll have trouble keeping it long term!

When you're coming up with your routine stacks, don't worry about how big or small you think the goal or routine is—you can use this framework for *any* goal, no matter the size!

Chapter 10 Action Steps

1. Create your routine stacking plan for the quarter.
2. Determine when you're going to track your goals and how.

3. Share any of your goals with me! I'd love to see one of your plans. Post a picture on your social media and tag me on Instagram @apurposedrivenmom so I can see it!

Chapter 11

Incentives and Obstacles

Now that we've talked about your vision and how to create a breakdown for your goals, let's chat about some of the fun things to add into your goal action plan to help make them stick.

I used to think that if I struggled with a goal, it just wasn't meant to be or I was unmotivated. But what I realized was that my way of looking at goals was missing a few steps and components to help me complete it.

Pre-Identifying Your Obstacles

Let's have some real talk right now.

There will be a moment while you are working on your goals where you are not going to feel like doing it.

It's human nature. You're going to hit a roadblock. An obstacle will threaten to toss you off course. Or you just plain won't feel motivated.

So instead of being surprised when it happens, let's troubleshoot and think of what might potentially happen in advance and make a plan for when it pops up.

Before you start to tackle your goal, I suggest taking a piece of paper (or use the action plan guide) and splitting it in half. On one side, jot down all the potential obstacles you might hit when facing a specific goal. Here are some examples:

- Not feeling motivated
- Getting behind
- Kids get sick
- Unsupportive spouse
- Just plain tired

List all the things you know will potentially derail you. Then, on the other side, come up with strategies to help push you through when you do get derailed.

If you know that the snooze button is an obstacle for you getting up for your morning routine, you could write down that you will move your phone across the room so you have to get up to hit the alarm (and while you're up, you might as well get going).

Maybe you know that you want to save money but get thrown off during the holidays. Your strategy could be to start a sinking fund where you save $20 a week all year so that by the end of the year, you've got the money saved and don't need to lean on credit cards.

What if your obstacle is you and that voice in your head? The one that tells you that you can't do it or makes you feel like you can procrastinate for later? What do you do then?

This is exactly what happened to me the morning I wrote this chapter. I was training for a half marathon. I used to run all the time BK (before kids) and know that it's one of those things that I love to do just for me. But it's hard. And I am ten years older than I was the last time I was running half marathons and completing Tough Mudder races.

There are many mornings where the alarm goes off and it's time to run, and I just don't want to do it. That morning was one of those.

I heard that voice in my head tell me that I could sleep in and that I would just skip today. That voice replayed a familiar negative spiral reminding me that I wasn't strong enough to finish this run and since it was longer than normal, I couldn't physically do it.

Luckily, I had already used some of my own strategies and pre-identified my obstacles—and knew this would happen. I had tools in my toolbox ready to combat that voice.

The lock screen of my phone often holds affirmations that remind me how capable I am of my goals, and I keep it there for just such moments. I pushed the little light on my phone and started to read them over and over.

"You are a runner."

"You can do this."

"You deserve to take the time to take care of you."

"Don't listen to the doubt."

By the time I had read through them three times, I was more awake and less scared. I got myself out of my bed and started to get ready for my run.

Because I knew that I'd have doubts (like everyone else), I prepared myself for them. Planning around your obstacles isn't about being pessimistic and planning to fail. It's about creating a realistic plan to set you up for success, even on the hard days!

I suggest taking time to create your own affirmations as well. You probably see affirmations all over the place. They are on coffee cups, notepads, and almost any site you go to on the internet. But I want to point out a problem I see with a lot of these affirmations:

They are coming from a fixed mindset rather than a growth mindset.

A fixed mindset is the belief that you are one way—either you're born that way or that is just the way you are now.

Affirmations that are more "fixed mindset" affirmations may be things like

"I am strong."

"I am a millionare."

"I am beautiful."

These affirmations also come from a "fake it 'til you make it" mentality. And while I don't think they are the worst way to use affirmations, I want to encourage you to make yours from a growth mindset.

A growth mindset comes from the perspective that through effort, things can change for you. It's the idea that you won't always be stuck in the same place and that change is possible. A growth mindset actually can start to change the neuropathways in your brain to believe you are a certain way. I won't get too sciency on you right now, but trust me, it's possible to change your brain and your belief system when you have a growth mindset.

So instead of creating affirmations that are just implying you've already "arrived" or that you are that way no matter what, create them using the "Even if, I can still . . ." method.

"Even if I am struggling today, I can still try my hardest."

"Even if I yell at my kids, I can still work to be a more patient mom."

"Even if I don't feel very strong right now, I can still work to get stronger."

These statements allow your belief system to change and grow with you. These types of affirmations start to delete that perfectionist mentality (either I am strong or I am not) and leave room for growth and mistakes. They leave room for you to just be an imperfect human working on themselves.

Using Incentives to Keep Going

I was the type of kid who would do anything for a sticker. And I find that those types of kids become the adults to write things down after they do them just so they can cross them off. You too?

I know that when we get started on our goals and our plans, we want to rely on our willpower and our why to get us through, but as we've talked about in previous chapters, it's not always enough.

I love to tie incentives to my goal plans because motivation is a muscle. And incentives help be an external motivator while our internal motivation muscle grows. Adding an incentive or two into your plan can help you continue on your way when you're unmotivated and keep you going when you want to quit.

For some reason, people can get really down on using rewards or incentives when it comes to goals (or even with our kids), but as a former special education teacher who specifically taught students with behavioral and emotional disabilities, I can tell you that external rewards that reinforce positive behaviors can be key in making things stick. There is nothing wrong with having a little bit of a bonus prize for yourself along the way—heck, you deserve it!

So, how do you determine what incentives you want?

Before you start your action plan, brainstorm a list of things that you want to reward yourself with when you complete your goal—whether it's a numerical, project-based or routine-based goal.

When you come up with your list, make sure not to write down things that would be counterintuitive to your goals.

For example, if you're working on a health or weight loss goal, you don't want your incentive to be dinner out at your guilty pleasure restaurant. If your goal is around finances, your goal might not be something you buy but instead time to yourself or an extended bubble bath.

Once you've picked the goal you want to work toward, let's look at it in a similar way we looked at a numerical goal and break it down for yourself.

I did this process when I completed the Whole30 one month. The Whole30 is an elimination diet which helps with inflammation, and since I was dealing with hormonal imbalances, I wanted to give it a try to see if it would help. But here is the thing: it's hard. Really hard. If you've ever done the Whole30, you know what I mean! I knew that I would need to bring in all the reinforcements to complete the thirty days—even though my why was strong and it was an important goal to me.

So, I found my incentive! Walmart had these cute little boots I wanted to treat myself to, so I picked them to be my Whole30 prize. Thankfully for me, they were $29.95, so it made my breakdown simple.

Since this program was thirty days long, I decided that for every day I completed Whole30, I would put a dollar into an envelope to go towards my boots fund. At the start of the month, I went to the bank and got $30 in singles so that I was prepared and had change each day.

Now, could I have just gone to Walmart and gotten the boots? Sure. And do I need to earn buying myself something. Not at all. But I knew that this could be a great way to help push me when days were hard. There is something magical about crossing the day off and physically moving money into my envelope. (I encourage you to use cash for yours too! Keeping the money in your account and just going to the store at the end of the month just isn't the same!)

Each night after my last meal, I would move the money into my envelope and track how much I had, and at the end of the thirty days, I felt so proud of myself as I walked in and got those boots. It wasn't just about the money. It was about showing up for myself, and that's what the boots represented.

I suggest you do the same thing for one of your quarterly goals. Pick your prize and divide up how much money you need (if it's a prize that costs something) and see how much you'd need to put aside either each day or each time you do a task. For example, if you have a goal of decluttering three times a week for twelve weeks, you wouldn't divide by the days in your goal plan (around ninety days for the quarter) but instead the days you plan to do tasks (thirty-six days of tasks).

You may have to put fifty cents into a jar each time or $5 depending on the price of your incentive. Head to the bank before you begin and create a secret space for your money that won't tempted you to take it (or your kids to find it). Not having the correct change is an easy way to stop tracking, and then this tool goes flying out your goal toolbox.

To make it a habit, put an alarm on your phone each night to remember to check in, track, and reward yourself. And as you put the money in, repeat one of the affirmations you picked that you know will help with your obstacles.

Each day I tracked and put my $1 in the envelope during Whole30, I would say to myself "I am becoming a healthier version of myself" or "I am worth this challenge" and it helped instill the goal and grow my pride and confidence.

Chapter 11 Action Steps

1. Looking at your goal plan, pre-identify a few obstacles that might come up and decide on a plan to proactively combat them.
2. Pick your prize and incentive for your upcoming goals.

Chapter 12

Creating a Community and Support System for Your Goals

When it comes to your support system, something interesting happens when you start going after your goals.

Sometimes people are super excited for you and get on board. Sometimes they might sabotage you (intentionally or unintentionally) or disappoint you because of their lack of support or excitement around your goal.

From the ages of sixteen to twenty-six, I had a drinking problem. I struggled a lot during my teens and into my twenties with my self-worth, and I would end up eating and drinking away my problems. I became known as the party girl in my friend circles—and I didn't mind it one bit.

I struggled my entire life with feeling like I mattered, and honestly, I felt like I was invisible. I didn't care what people said about me (and a lot of it wasn't very nice) as long as they were talking about me, because if they were talking about me, at least they knew I existed.

One weekend, after a long and drunken weekend club hopping where I had almost broken my hand because I punched the bathroom door and threatened to fight anyone else trying to help me, I realized enough was enough. I had to pause and stop drinking for a while to get my life together. I was a school teacher during the day and then spent my weekends blacking out so that I could escape my depression and my self-hatred. And I was tired.

I remember crying to a friend telling her how I felt and that I needed to stop going out with them for a while and take care of me.

And I'll never forget her response. It wasn't "How can I help?" or "I am so sorry you feel like this." Instead, she told me, "It's really not as bad as you're making it seem, and honestly, I'm just worried that we won't ever see you anymore if you stop drinking."

Because all we did was go out to drink—it had become our entire group identity. So instead of a supportive response, she basically confirmed the thoughts I already had: if I didn't show up as a party girl, I had no value.

I took the next few years after that weekend away from drinking until I got to a place where I felt comfortable having a glass of wine or two for enjoyment and not because I wanted to hide or mask my feelings or myself.

But that conversation has played in my head over and over. And maybe you've had a similar experience.

You tell your girlfriends you want to save money, but they always suggest super expensive girls nights out. You want to eat healthier, but your partner brings your favorite junk food into the house. You are trying to make sure you leave work at a reasonable time, but a coworker (who you told your goal to) has a habit of dropping off things that are last minute and "must be done tonight."

Let's be clear though—no one else is responsible for your success. That's up to you. But it makes it a heck of a lot easier if you have a supportive community around yourself.

So, why do people not seem to support your goals?

A reason you might not think about is fear. A lot of times people may not be as supportive of your goals as you'd like (whether they sabotage you or just don't seem to be the cheerleader you want) because they are afraid of what will happen if you achieve your goals.

I see this happen a lot in the entrepreneurial space with my mom friends and the moms I coach. They start their business, and their partner doesn't seem to get behind them in the way they expect and need. Some of the lack of support is coming from that partner's own fear and what-if mentality.

"What if this is successful and she has less time for the family (and more gets put on my plate)?"

"What if she makes more money than I do and doesn't need me?"

"What if she finds happiness in this business and it makes her happier that I do?"

Our partners won't always tell us their lack of support comes from fear (and honestly, they might not even realize it), but it can play out in ways such as them giving you a hard time about the time you spend on work or questioning every financial decision you make for your business.

The second reason your current support system might not step up like you'd like for your goals is because it puts a mirror back on them.

I know now that the reason my friend might not have been as encouraging when I wanted to stop drinking is because my acknowledging a problem put a mirror back up to her about how her drinking could have been a problem too.

One of my clients was having a similar struggle when it came to her weight loss. She told her friends her goals, and they seemed excited but always make her feel guilty at restaurants because everyone always got dessert but her. A few weeks later, her friend confided in her that she was worried that if she lost the weight, she'd be the only overweight friend left in their group and would feel super alone.

Oftentimes our success—whether it's decluttering our home or running a marathon—can make others feel less than.

We can't let other people's feelings about our goals stop us or make us feel guilty about working toward something important to us. We also can't always blame them for not being as on board as we need.

Finding Your Support Community

I suggest you find external accountability and a support system to be your community while you're going after your goals, particularly if your current one isn't on board. I don't think you need to ditch your current friend group if they aren't as supportive as you need (remember, it's *your* goal and not everyone is going to care about it like you do), but it's super helpful to add some cheerleaders into your corner.

I know it can be challenging to find friends as a busy mom, but trust me, your people are out there! You don't need to have a huge group to get the accountability that you need!

I knew that I was going to need some support when I created my goal to increase my water intake. I don't know about you, but I struggle to get in the amount of water I need each day. The days get super busy and oftentimes coffee calls my name way before I even think about drinking water.

I mentioned this casually to a friend of mine and she suggested we text each other throughout the day every time we drank water. We kept this up for a few weeks until it really became a habit. Just the simple check-ins and texts were a reminder for each of us to stop, drop, and chug that water!

When you're looking for an accountability partner or group, remember that it's not one sided. I've been in way too many groups where I wind up being the only one sending check-ins or emails, but no one is checking in on me. Those groups or partnerships are typically the ones that fizzle out because one person gets tired of always doing check-ins.

If you have a local group of mom friends, you might also want to lean on them for support. I know lots of moms who make appointments to meet up at the park a few times a week to go walking and chat. The fact that other people are waiting on you can be that little push you need to work on your goals when you don't really feel like it.

I used a small group accountability system like this when it came to a reading and growth goal. I have a small group of friends from my old church where we would meet biweekly to complete a Bible study on racial reconciliation and the church. We knew that it was an important topic we all wanted to carve out time to learn about and discuss, but without those other five members reading the same book and engaging in discussion with me, I don't know if I would have really prioritized that time to learn and grow.

If you can't find people locally to connect with, I suggest searching online for a great group! I know social media can be either a distraction or an energy-suck, but there is a way to use it for good! You can find a Facebook group on pretty much any topic for any goal you are working on. Facebook groups are where I've met so many of my closest friends because we were going after similar goals and created a group message thread to check in.

You can either outright ask inside the group to see if anyone is interested in teaming up because they have a similar goal, or you can hang in the group for a while until you find people you vibe with and ask them. I know that if I post in a group (that allows it) that I want to connect with others around a goal, I might get a ton of comments but only a handful of people ever actually participate, and honestly, I just might not get along with some of them.

If you create a group or support community online and it fizzles or doesn't work out the first time, don't give up! You'll find your community and people! If you want to connect in my group, just search Purpose Driven Mom Community on Facebook and you'll find thousands of other positive goal-chasing moms to hang with!

Creating Your Support Community at Home

I know we've talked a lot about finding a community outside of your home—but don't forget about your people! A lot of times I lean on my friends or online community for accountability because let's be honest, my husband doesn't have the same level of care or buy-in for every little goal I'm going after. But that doesn't mean we don't share our goals with each other!

I think it's key to enroll your family in your vision for your goals—and hear what they'd like to achieve too. Conversation in our home is often centered around our goals whether it's me writing this book or my daughter wanting to learn how to ride her bike without her training wheels. If it's something someone is excited to accomplish, we share it with each other!

If you have a goal you're going after, by sharing it with your family, they can help be part of your support system. You can let them know what it would look like to support your goals and how they can help. When I started writing the book, I shared this goal with my husband and my kids and told them why it was so important to me.

I knew writing a book was going to take more time and focus, so I let them know that a way they can help this goal is when Mommy is in the office for writing time, you need to make sure to stay on the other side of the door and go to Daddy when you need something (because Daddy can open those fruit snacks too, right?). I also told my husband that if I was going to go on a book tour, it might take me away from the family for a few days at a time, and we talked about what that would look like and what support he might need to make that happen.

Maybe you have a finance goal and want to pay off your car loan by the end of the quarter or save up for a trip to Disney. If you let the kids know what the goal is, why it matters, and how they can help, they might be more invested and supportive.

Every time you're at the store and they ask for something, you can remind them that instead of buying that toy, the dollar is going into the Disney Jar for the trip. When you get home, you can have them put the money in the jar. Or if you're saving money online, have them color in a tracker to show how much you've saved.

Remember, while your family might not understand your goal in the way you want them to and might give you some push back when you work on it, by enrolling them in the goal and telling them why it matters, you're adding another layer of support and another tool in your goals toolbox for when times get tough!

Chapter 12 Action Steps

1. Start to find your support community for the quarter—whether it's one person or a group.
2. Search Purpose Driven Mom Community on Facebook and come join our group! We'd love to be in your corner!

PILLAR #4

ROUTINES

Chapter 13

Routines to Support Your Goals

I'm super excited for you. If you've made it this far to the book, I hope you're starting to feel empowered and excited about how you can take back control of your time without overwhelm or burnout. So far, we've talked about how time blocking will help you create the base for your goals and how quarterly planning will let you gain progress even when life throws you curveballs.

We're now moving into the fourth pillar of the 15 Minute Formula, and that's routines.

I love routines. I thrive on routines.

But before we dive too much into your day-to-day routines, let's talk about routines to support your goals.

I never made any routines around my goals. I would make my goals, make a great action plan for them, and do my best to follow it. If the plan didn't work out, I would simply try the exact same plan again, hoping my willpower and motivation would be different this time around.

Of course, it wasn't. And I found myself with the same goals (decluttering my house or finally getting my health in order) on my vision board year after year.

Have you been there too?

We all have!

Why don't we stop and question *why* we are doing it? What sense does it make to keep doing the same thing and hoping it'll work?

That's why you need to make sure you add in routines *around* your goals. Because our goals are moving things—they can change and ebb and flow. We just have to have a great system in place to make them work!

Why Tracking Matters

Peter Drucker is credited to have said, "If you can't measure it, you can't improve it." and I couldn't agree more!

If you aren't tracking your goals, how will you know how well you are actually doing? If you rely just on how you feel around a goal, it's easy to either underestimate or overestimate your progress.

I first noticed this on some of my group coaching calls with my membership The Purpose Driven Mom Club. I would ask the members how their week went, and almost immediately, they would list all the things they didn't do.

Have you ever done that before? Your partner comes home from work and asks about your day and your first response is a rattling of what didn't happen?

When we base our progress off just emotions, it can be hard to feel confident that we're making any progress or know what's working and what isn't.

If you're going to go through all the steps to create a quarterly plan, you should take the time to track things as well!

But tracking your goals can feel like a goal in itself. It's something you need to remember to do and a routine you have to add into your day until it becomes second nature to complete check-ins periodically on your goals.

How Should You Track Your Goals?

If you're going to make tracking a routine, I suggest you do it often. I think that doing nightly, weekly, monthly, and quarterly goal tracking will help you stay on top of your goals.

The more you check in with your goals, the more you are reminded of them. There are weeks where I complete all of my tracking routines and might not accomplish much when it comes to the actual goals.

And I am okay with that. The fact that I am checking in on them regularly reminds me of what I said I wanted to work on and my vision. If I stopped checking in on my goals because I wasn't accomplishing what I wanted to, it would be so easy for me to forget about a goal I set for myself or continue to put that goal on the back burner.

When it comes to tracking, you want to keep it simple so you can have the data. We'll talk about what to do with your data and tracking as the month goes on, but in the simplest way, going through a checklist of "Did I complete this or not?" can help you stay focused.

If you've gone ahead and created a detailed quarterly plan, you should know exactly what to work on and how to stay on track.

Each day when you sit down to check in on how things went, comb through your original plan, marking down what got accomplished and what did not. This is a simple yes/no inventory. There is no emotion in your tracking, and this is not the place to shame yourself for what you didn't accomplish.

I want to caution you on putting too much meaning behind your tracking right now.

You are more than your to-do list. You are more than your action plan. Having a day where you didn't accomplish all you set out to do does not make you any less worthy as a person, and having a day where you complete everything does not make you any better.

We use these tracking lists for data. We're using this to see your progress and celebrate you showing up.

We have a saying we use in my community: "Showing up is progress." So, whether you show up by completing your goal that day or show up simply by tracking what happened, be proud of that progress and the fact that you're not throwing in the towel and giving up.

At the end of most days, I have a list of things that I didn't accomplish when it comes to my goals. I don't want to forget these things, so I take the things that didn't get done and highlight them in my planner and then pull them off the current day and put them on a large Post-it Note I keep paperclipped on the top of the planner so I can see what needs to get done.

I also quickly decided whether I want to put those tasks on the next day or fit them elsewhere in my week. Depending on whether my goal is sequential or not, I may have to make adjustments to other goals for that week. If the goal isn't something that has to be completed in a certain order, I take the task that was missed and add it to my thought catcher time (Review this in Chapter 5) that I've scheduled for myself. Because here is the thing: I know I'm going to get behind. I know I'll miss stuff. But because I have thought catcher time, I'm not going to stress about when it'll get done. I've given myself that buffer for life to happen.

A Note on Daily Tracking

I used to think that I had to do my tracking at night but was struggling each evening to remember to track. By the end of the night, I was burnt out and didn't feel like tracking and would just forget.

I started to mix it up and track in the mornings. I knew that I was more refreshed in the mornings and excited to check in on my goals. I created a new part of my morning routine: while I had my breakfast, I would open up my goal board that I made using the Trello website.

Now instead of feeling awful because I couldn't remember to check in each night with my goals and giving up on tracking altogether, I customized the routine to work for me! Make sure to do the same for you and find a time that works best. Put a timer on your phone to help make it a habit and track away.

Your Ta-Da List

While I know I just said we need to take the emotion out of tracking so we can look at the data, there is a daily tracking routine that I think will help you gain momentum, and that is your Ta-Da list.

I know we all love our to-do lists, but often they leave us

feeling inadequate and like a failure. I think it's important to be realistic and track how things are going so that we can pivot our goals and stay the course. But what if we also added in a place where you can be a cheerleader for yourself?

You can create this list inside your planner, make a separate notebook just for these Ta-Das or write it in the notepad of your phone—just make sure you put it down somewhere!

When you're finished with your yes/no tracking for the day, take a minute to write down three things you are proud of accomplishing that day. These could be things ranging from "I washed, folded, *and* put away the laundry in one day" (I know, wouldn't it be a miracle?) to "I spent twenty minutes on a passion project," to "I had one-on-one time with my kids."

There is no right or wrong with what you jot down, but the point is that you acknowledge and show yourself some gratitude for showing up—whatever that looks like!

Weekly Tracking and Checking In on Your Goals

If you start making daily tracking a habit, then your weekly tracking should only take fifteen minutes or less. The goal of weekly tracking is to celebrate your success, see your progress, and adjust any goals so that you can still hit your deadline.

Weekly tracking is what helped me complete the writing of this book in just four months—which was the original goal.

I knew that I could conquer putting this book together in four months if I used my own systems, and weekly tracking helped me stay on course.

Once I realized that I wanted the book to be around 50,000 words, I used the numerical goal-setting system to break down how many words I needed to write each day to complete it. I added in my own buffer days so that I was making it a goal to write three to four times a week for one hour (since I did an inventory and knew I could write 1,000–1,500 words in an hour on average).

Since I knew how many days I needed to write a week in order to stay on track, at the start of each week, I would plan out my writing days and track them like a daily goal. Then on Sundays, while I was making my plan for the week, I would check in on my progress and see if I accomplished what I set out to do.

If I missed a writing day, got behind or even ahead on my writing, I knew that in order to keep my original four-month deadline, I would have to adjust things. Therefore, I changed up my numbers and the goal each week.

I suggest you do this every Sunday as you get ready to go into the week. In Chapter 14 we'll talk about weekly planning and the entire process for it. For now, let's just do the first part, which is the weekly tracking.

Check over the goals you had set for the week and create a list of "Weekly Success" and "Areas of Growth." Write down all the things you did accomplish whether it was the first part of your morning routine stack or reading two chapters of a book. Don't forget to hype yourself up as you write it down and say your positive affirmations that remind you that you are moving closer to that person you want to be.

For any tasks that didn't get completed, let's not just leave them! Instead, go through the process to adjust the goal according to how many weeks or days you have left.

For example, if you had a numerical goal to read fifty pages of a book a week and you completed twenty pages this week (way to go!), in order to keep on track and finish your book at the end of the month, you need to make some small adjustments. Instead of saying "Oh, I'll just add twenty pages to Monday" (which we know can overwhelm you and leave you wanting to give up as you get more and more behind), just redo your math.

Book Pages = 200

Pages Read = 20

Pages to Read (in 3 weeks) = 180

180 pages / 3 weeks = 60 pages a week

60 pages / 5 days a week = 12 pages a day

By adjusting the goal each week, your goal simply went from ten pages a day to twelve, which is much more manageable to our brains and our schedules.

If you don't do this process with your goals each week, your goals will start to really stack up, and small adjustments soon become big ones as you get to the end of the month and realize you have five days to read 150 pages!

Monthly Goal Tracking and the Reflection Pyramid

The monthly goal-tracking system is so important to add into your goal routines even when you have months that feel off or where you didn't accomplish as much as you'd like.

We've been talking a lot about taking the emotions out of your goals so that you can look at the numbers and the data, but when we reflect and track for the month, we're going to bring all the feelings back.

Because here is the thing: your feelings aren't bad. You need to feel them. You need to identify them, and it's important to ask yourself how the month felt for you.

But you can't just rely solely on the feelings. Often when I get with my coaching clients and ask how their month went, they'll tell me about the last bad thing that happened and all they didn't accomplish, and it isn't until we complete the Reflection Pyramid that we get a truthful assessment about how things went and why they might have gone that way.

At the close of each month, complete a similar tracking as you would each week. Pull out and celebrate your successes and readjust any quarterly goals for the next few months. Sometimes, you might want to change up the next few months' themes to make sure you're giving yourself adequate time to complete things, and sometimes you might choose to prolong the deadline for a given goal.

I use a Trello board for this (and you can snag this template with your 30-Day Action Guide), but you could keep a journal specifically for this reflection process. I love to keep documentation with how things are going so that in a few months when I look back, I can see the success and growth I've had and also acknowledge some of the hard things I've been through and came out stronger because of.

Once you've done your data-based tracking and updating of your goals, let's talk through how your month felt for you by using the Reflection Pyramid. Again, a journal is a great place to write this out. I suggest when you do this, you grab your planner so you can look back into your month and jog some memories.

reflection pyramid

1	LESSON YOU LEARNED
2	THINGS YOU'RE PROUD OF
3	POINTS OF GRATITUDE
4	HARD PARTS
5	HIGHLIGHTS

5 Highlights of Your Month

Let's start with identifying the best parts of your month! These could be fun things you did, times where you hit your goals, or anything you determine as your monthly highlight. Make sure you come up with five. I know it feels easier to talk about the negative things that happen, but I am challenging you to find five—even if it's just that you got a shower alone!

4 Monthly Struggles

As we go up the pyramid, we want to take some time to identify things that were a struggle for you this month. This will help you see any correlation to goals you struggled with but also serve as documentation of things that happened. I love looking back and seeing how much progress I have made over time, even when things were a struggle.

I remember looking back a year later at a struggle I documented one January. I was having a hard time with my stepson and just felt like we couldn't connect and kept butting heads. I wrote on my board that one of my struggles was our relationship. You couldn't even imagine the smile on my face in December when I read that and realized by the end of the year our relationship had taken a 180-degree turn, and we were so much closer!

3 Things You're Grateful For

I love anchoring in gratitude, and it's one of those things that, after writing down your struggles, you might need to see that things aren't that bad (even when they feel it). Writing down pieces of gratitude isn't meant to cross off the things that were hard or the struggles you had—remember, all of your feelings are valid and real. Anchoring your month into gratitude is meant to remind you of things that are going well in your life—even when you might not feel it.

2 Moments You're Proud Of

We complete this monthly reflection process in my membership The Purpose Driven Mom Club (Head to www.

apurposedrivenmom.com/club to learn more and join us!) together as a group, and I find that the moms in my community struggle with identifying this section the most.

It can be really challenging to think of things that you are proud of and even harder for us to say it to ourselves. I push you in this section each month to think of two things *you* did that were amazing—not your kids or your family—but you.

Did you stick to a goal? Show up for a commitment to yourself? Keep calm more than normal? Whatever it is, write it down and then say it out loud. Tell yourself you're proud of yourself for it and cheer yourself on!

1 Lesson You Learned

Each month you'll learn something—whether it's a good or hard lesson. After you've gone through your reflection process and really looked at how the month went data- and numbers-wise and how it went feelings-wise, ask yourself, "What is something I've learned?"

These could be lessons such as "It's okay to ask for help" or "I get stressed out when I don't get enough sleep" or even "If I don't track my goals, I tend to forget about them day to day."

Whatever your lesson is, write it down and think about how you can put it into action next month.

Adjusting Your Plan After the Quarter

Hopefully by the end of the quarter, tracking has become a new habit for you and you're able to look at how things have gone and make adjustments to stay on course.

But can we be honest?

It's not all going to stay on course.

You are going to have goals you go after and don't accomplish. Your big plans for the quarter are likely to get derailed. Things pop up as moms that throw our good intentions off course, and that's okay.

Before we jump into reflecting on the quarter and what happened and what didn't, make sure you take a second to remember that there is no shame in not crossing it all off your to-do list. It's okay that it all didn't get accomplished, and you are no less worthy because of it.

Deep breath.

Okay, now that we're on the same page about how awesome you are—let's take a second to adjust the rest of the yearly plan.

Schedule in your calendar thirty minutes to reflect on your current twelve-week quarter (remember, this doesn't have to line up with a calendar perfectly, just the twelve weeks you decide) and begin to adjust and plan for the next quarter.

I suggest that you start with your list of wins from the quarter and areas of growth. Since you've hopefully been doing all of your tracking, this shouldn't take too long to come up with and you'll be left with an awesome list to celebrate.

Now that you know where you got off track (I don't love the use of the word "behind"—I mean, who decides what "behind" actually is? And doesn't "behind" make you feel awful? Let's replace it with the word "off track," shall we?), you can use a similar process that we used during the weekly and monthly reflections to determine how things will go for the rest of the year.

First up, let's adjust your numerical goals since they are the ones that are most likely to be completed over the course of twelve months and can easily be adjusted.

For example, if I made a goal to read twenty-four books over the course of the year and predetermined that I should complete six of those books in the first quarter of my year but only read three, I know I'll have to make adjustments to still hit my goal.

Using the adjustment process makes this simple math and helps my goal feel less overwhelming as the year goes on.

Goal = 24 books
Read = 3 books
Books to Read = 21 books
Time Left to Read = 8 months
21 books / 8 months = 2.65 books per month

Now you'll make some simple adjustments and instead of reading two books a month, your new goal is a little over two and a half books. Since you've made those adjustments, it's a lot easier to manage than if you waited until the end of the year and realized you had twenty-one books to go and only a month to complete it. This is why I suggest you also do this process monthly. It makes it so much easier when you complete the quarterly reflection and audit.

When it comes to your project-based quarterly goals, we'll use a little different process. If you followed my quarterly planning system, you most likely already determined your themes for the next few twelve-week periods, so before you try to shove this quarter's goals in, ask yourself a few questions:

- Do the goals I got behind on fit into my theme for the next quarter?
- Do they need to be completed before the next quarter's goals begin?
- Are they still a top micro priority for this season of life?
- Is there a better time of year where they might fit?

If after asking yourself these questions you determine that you can move this goal to another quarter, go for it! Adjust when you'll work on it and be ready to create your plan during that twelve-week period. Remember, no guilt about this! Just because something made sense for one quarter but didn't get completed and was moved doesn't mean you're giving up on your goals. It means you're making priority-based decisions based on your life!

If you determine that you want to add it into the next twelve-week plan, get ready to make a few adjustments so you don't overwhelm yourself. A mistake I've made in the past is deciding that I will move something into the next quarter by just adding it to my list. I would then get behind on the list I planned and that goal and just quit because I felt like I would never get it done.

If you're going to keep that project-based goal, make some simple adjustments so that you're not adding too much to your list. You can do this by simply adding in one extra task to your goals time block each day or carving out extra time on the weekend. You can also double up your tasks for your goals so that you can work on one at a time.

You have the power to make your plan flexible and to work for you!

Using a Goal Audit When You Get Off Track

I used to be one of those people who had Groundhog's Day goals. You know the type, right? When you write them on your plan for the week, something happens, you blame yourself for not "wanting it badly enough," vow to try again later, and just put the exact same goal and plan on your schedule for the following week.

Rinse and repeat. Over and over again.

Finally, after years of realizing this was not going to be the way I'd make any progress toward any of my goals, I decided to figure out *why* my goals weren't working. This isn't something we talk about a lot—*why* something doesn't work.

It's easy to just jump in and blame our busy lives or our laziness, but as I've been reminding you throughout the book, it's not that anything is wrong with you, it's just that you need some adjustments to your plan.

Once a month when I am doing my monthly goal reflections, I look back and see which goals didn't make as much progress as I'd hoped and do what I call a goal audit.

The primary purpose of a goal audit is to become a detective about your goal to figure out why something isn't working and then adjust it to set yourself up for success moving forward in the next month, week, or quarter.

By adding a routine of goal auditing into your month, you'll start to make your goals moveable and work for you better—instead of just dropping them because they feel impossible at the time.

Questions to Ask Yourself During Your Goal Audit

Let's walk through the goal auditing process together. Pick a goal that you've been trying to meet for what seems like forever but you've struggled with—this is the perfect type of goal to audit. You know it's important to you, you want to achieve it, but something just doesn't seem to be clicking and you're struggling with inaction.

goal audit

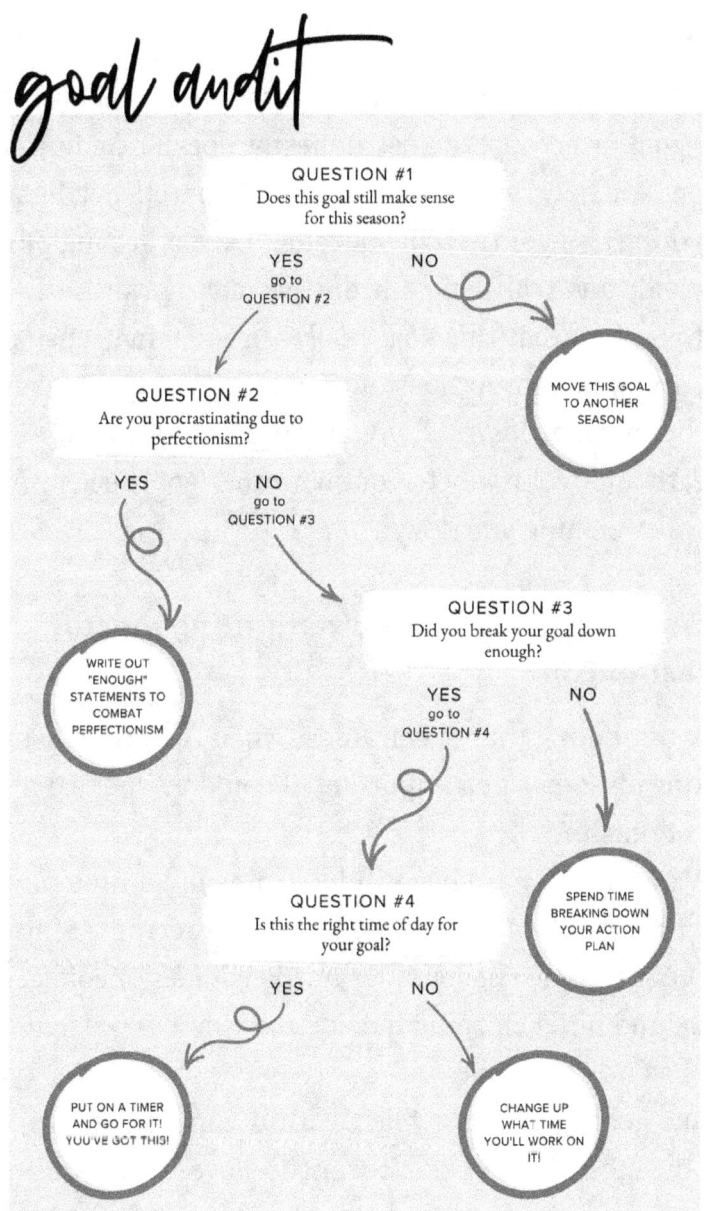

QUESTION #1
Does this goal still make sense
for this season?

YES
go to
QUESTION #2

NO

QUESTION #2
Are you procrastinating due to
perfectionism?

MOVE THIS GOAL
TO ANOTHER
SEASON

YES

NO
go to
QUESTION #3

WRITE OUT
"ENOUGH"
STATEMENTS TO
COMBAT
PERFECTIONISM

QUESTION #3
Did you break your goal down
enough?

YES
go to
QUESTION #4

NO

QUESTION #4
Is this the right time of day for
your goal?

SPEND TIME
BREAKING DOWN
YOUR ACTION
PLAN

YES

NO

PUT ON A TIMER
AND GO FOR IT!
YOU'VE GOT THIS!

CHANGE UP
WHAT TIME
YOU'LL WORK ON
IT!

Question #1 *Does this goal still make sense for this season?*

One of the reasons that you may struggle with taking action on a goal is because it just honestly doesn't fit into your season. You may really, really want to accomplish it, but with everything else going on in your life, it keeps getting pushed to the side and truly isn't one of your micro priorities.

If you find that this goal really isn't making sense right now, give yourself permission to add it to another quarter. Just by moving this goal, you'll most likely be able to take a breath and feel ready to conquer other goals because this one was weighing you down.

Question #2 *Are you procrastinating due to perfectionism?*

Did you know that oftentimes when we procrastinate working on something important, it could be due to our own perfectionism?

We want to have a beautiful morning quiet time routine, but our kids often wake up early and interrupt. Since it's not the picture we have in our heads with a hot coffee, cozy couch, and birds chirping outside the window, we figure we might as well not do it.

Our goal boards are filled with dreams of starting our own business, but we don't want to have to work at night when the kids go to bed, so we decide we'll just try again later when they are at school. We don't have the perfect work schedule, so we keep putting our dreams off.

Is this something you're doing? If it is, take note that your perfectionism might be getting in the way of going after your goals. Instead of waiting for the perfect time, write down a list of statements to help you combat that perfectionist mindset. Here are some examples:

- While I want quiet time for my Bible reading, I am still able to listen to the audio version while I make my kids breakfast.
- Even though I'd love to have my own workspace to grow my business, I am capable of getting started during nap time.
- I want to be a marathon runner, but I will applaud my efforts to finish that first mile.

By creating our own vision statements around what we are struggling with when it comes to perfectionism, we can bring to light how we're feeling stuck without staying in victim mode.

Question #3 Did I break my goal down enough?

As I talked about when I explained how to break down your goals, the goal breakdown is where the magic happens inside of your action plan. By creating a plan with tiny wins for your numerical, project-based, and routine goals, you'll be able to ditch the overwhelm when it comes to your big goals.

But if you're like many of the women I work with, you probably skipped that part.

Oh yes, I will tell them until I am blue in the face how by taking time to break down your goals, you are making it a million times easier to stick with your plan, but a lot of people won't do the work.

"I don't have time to break my goals down."

"When it's time to work, I'll just get started."

"I know what I have to do."

I hear you. And I believe you know what to do. But when it's time to actually work on things, our brains are overloaded. Decision fatigue is *so* real, and it can make it hard for our brain to focus and get started.

If you're auditing a goal that you realize you've been working on it for a long time and making little to no progress with, ask yourself Question #3.

This is exactly what happened to me when I was working on my Life Coach Certification. I shared this example with you earlier in the book, but now let me show you how I ran it through the goal audit process.

I had this goal on my quarterly board and realized that I was dragging the lessons from week to week and not accomplishing much. It was time to figure out why.

Question #1 Is it the right time?

Yup, this aligns with my business and the season I am in.

Question #2 Is this perfectionism?

Nope. I'm okay with not having the ideal learning environment to get it done.

Question #3 Did I break it down enough?

Ding. Ding. Ding. We have a winner!

I realized that while I had written down which modules I would take each week, I wasn't specific enough about the lessons. For this particular certification, there were ten different modules and each module had anywhere from five to nine lessons inside of it.

I thought I would just be able to say to myself, "The goal is to complete the module by the end of the week," and it would be fine since I was super motivated to finish this goal.

But it wasn't enough.

I went back to the drawing board and broke down each week with exactly which lessons I would watch on which days. I even buffered in time to take notes, complete extension items, and work on assignments—which was not something I had planned in the beginning. Because as I went through my audit, I realized that I was looking at the modules and my brain was saying "Nope, this will take too long," and I would just put it off until the next day.

My new plan consisted of fifteen to thirty minutes, five days a week of work for the next six weeks. I could do fifteen minutes. I could convince my brain of fifteen minutes. I could get started for just fifteen minutes and be done.

By adjusting and auditing my goal and creating a new breakdown for it, I was able to complete the certification earlier than planned without feeling so overwhelmed by the task.

Question #4 Is this the right time of day for my goal?

The final question I'm going to suggest you ask yourself during your goal audit is if you planned to complete the goal at the right time of day?

This ties back to that perfectionism we talked about in Question #2. We often have this beautiful picture of what we want things to look like and, when it doesn't align, we struggle to move things around.

If you're finding you have a goal that is in the right season and is broken down enough, look at the time of day you planned to complete it and really think about whether that makes sense.

A client of mine was working on a morning exercise routine. She knew that she wanted to add more exercise and movement to her day, and from everything she's seen, it's best to do it in the mornings. She made a great goal to go walking four times a week before everyone else got up.

But after a week of trying this, she had missed all but one of her workouts.

What was happening?

Well, she was a mom of a two-month-old baby who still wasn't sleeping through the night. Most mornings when her alarm went off, she had just fallen back to sleep after a nursing session and was just way too tired. Because she wasn't able to work out in the mornings, she would roll over, tell herself she'd try again tomorrow, and then feel awful about missing it.

When I brought up the idea of moving her workout later in the afternoon, she said she had never thought about it. She follows a lot of Instagram influencers who talk about how we "must" get up earlier than our kids and have our own time to work out, so it never even crossed her mind as a possibility.

I suggested she wait until after breakfast and take the baby with her. I knew it wasn't ideal because she wanted time alone to take care of her, but moving the workout to take the baby with her was better than not doing it at all.

Over the course of a few months, the walks started to happen midday and became a routine. Now that the baby is almost a year old, she's been able to increase the intensity of her workouts and the baby joins in! They've created a great routine where the baby plays in her play area while mom streams workouts at home.

Just by allowing herself to move some things around timing-wise, she's gone above and beyond, and now exercise is a habit that she does daily—even with the baby around!

Chapter 13 Action Steps

1. Add into your planner when you'll do your daily, weekly, monthly, and quarterly goal tracking.
2. Put a timer on your phone to remind yourself to track daily!
3. Pick a goal that hasn't been working and put it through the goal audit. Adjust that goal to make more sense for you to take action on this week.

Chapter 14

Routines to Support Your Week

No matter how mapped out my goals and plans are, things tend to go awry. There are always moments where I feel a bit off or where life can get too overwhelming. And that's why I've created some basic routines that are now my lifeline as a busy mom.

We've talked so much about creating your schedule and mapping out your goals, but I think it's key to also talk about routines to add into your week to help when the burnout does start to set in and the overwhelm feels unbearable.

Like I mentioned earlier, as a school teacher, my schedule felt super-duper tight. I had to be at certain places every thirty minutes in my day, and there was no wiggle room for my goals. Even if I had planned out which personal goal I wanted to focus on, I often found myself struggling to figure out when I would fit things in.

When I became an entrepreneur and had the freedom to make my own schedule around my personal and family needs, it felt exciting because finally, I would be able to make it work. But it wasn't until I created a weekly planning system that I truly had the time freedom for my goals without feeling like I was just adding a million things to an already busy schedule.

The Best Weekly Planning System

Weekly planning is something that I teach in depth in my membership, The Purpose Driven Mom Club, and I would venture to say it's one of the club members' favorite parts of the week. We meet every single Sunday night to review our goals for the week and plan out the week ahead. Even on weeks moms feel behind or if they haven't shown up live in a while, getting on with other moms to even think about their week helps them feel centered and ready to take on the week and whatever challenges it brings.

If you've done the leg work that we've talked about in this book, including creating your time blocks and breaking down your goals, then weekly planning should be a breeze! If you haven't done those steps—no worries! You can implement this plan easily, though it may take a little bit longer!

There are five steps to the planning process:

1. Write in your appointments and blocks.
2. Time for your goals.

3. Stack your routines.
4. Add in time for learning.
5. Fill the rest up and pick your big 3.

When a lot of moms start planning, they most likely start with all the things that everyone else needs from them. I'm going to encourage you to stop and flip that on its head. If you're someone who has found themselves saying, "I don't have the time for my goals," I want to encourage you to try planning the 15 Minute Formula way and see what happens!

Step 1: Your Appointments and Blocks

While I know we said my planning system would have you starting with you first, but listen, we have responsibilities. As moms, a lot falls on our plates, and I don't know about you, but if I don't write it down, it doesn't happen.

Before we begin adding time for you, grab your planner and map out your time blocks for the week. Since time blocks can vary day to day or week to week, I like to do this each Sunday as a reminder of my schedule. I try to use different color highlighters for each block, but let's be real, that doesn't always happen! Don't let not having the perfect planner, pens, or markers keep you from getting started! I'm sure you have a ton of planners in your planner graveyard, but there is no perfect planner (at least I haven't found it yet). So, find the one that works the best for you or a notebook and get moving!

I like to map out my blocks so that I can see the themes I've set for myself in advance and try to create micro priorities within each block. Once you've mapped out your blocks, write down all of the appointments you can't miss. These can range from your work hours to sports and activities to doctor's appointments or coaching calls. Put them in now so you don't forget them and you can see what you truly "have" to do.

Step 2: Time for Your Goals

I know how overwhelming it can feel to find time for your goals, but (hopefully) you took the time to break down your goals and now know exactly what to do.

It's time to figure out when you're going to do it.

Before we add in all the tiny tasks for others—the Target runs, phone calls or things people want you to stop and drop to do—let's just put in fifteen minutes for your goals.

Yup, fifteen minutes.

That's all I am asking you to start with. Up until this point, you might have been thinking that you won't have time to implement that plan you made, but trust me, there is a reason we broke everything down into fifteen-minute chunks.

Because you can do fifteen minutes.

Can you do more? Sure, but let's start with fifteen minutes. As I mentioned earlier in the book, fifteen minutes can help grow your confidence and get your momentum moving. So for now, your second step in your weekly planning is to add in fifteen minutes a day for one of your goals.

Since you've themed your time blocks, the simplest way to do this is to find the time block that fits that goal and write it down. Make it an appointment with yourself and make it as detailed as you can.

You might write down that you're going to walk a mile during time block one on Mondays. On Tuesdays, you're going to spend fifteen minutes decluttering the kid's toys after the kids go to bed. And on Friday, you'll read chapter one of your new book during the naptime time block.

Make this date with yourself so you don't miss it. If you want to block out fifteen minutes a day per goal, go for it! But I find that starting small with just a tiny chunk for you is the best way to retrain your brain into believing it is possible for you to create time for your goals.

Remember also that each day can be different. Somedays you might be able to fit in 2–3 fifteen-minute chunks for your goals, and other days, you will be excited to get in one. There is no right or wrong here, but my only ask is if you can put in fifteen minutes for you each day because you deserve it.

Step 3: Stack Your Routines

Let's pull out those routine stacks from Chapter 9 and add them into your plan now! Since you've hopefully gone through the steps of creating the vision and stacks, you know exactly what to work on. Once you start adding in the weekly reflection routine, this part becomes a breeze because you'll know when you're ready to stack!

Inside your planner, write down which routine(s) you'll be focusing on for the week and what that stack looks like.

If you're just starting out, you might write down this:

Morning Routine:

- Yoga
- Breakfast
- Start laundry

Or if you've been doing it for a while, your routine might have stacked:

Morning Routine:

- Yoga
- Breakfast
- Start laundry
- Journaling
- Empty dishwasher
- Shower
- Daily cleaning

Remember that each week you get the chance to add to your stack if you're ready or keep it where it is. What is key here is that you write it down first. Make sure your routine is in your planner so that you can see it and the stack is super clear. In the beginning, the routine should take fifteen minutes or less so it's easy to sneak it in. As the length of the routine grows, your schedule will expand to find it all in!

Step 4: Add in Time for Learning

The final time for you I want to suggest you add in is fifteen minutes of learning a day.

Cue the eye roll. Come on, I know it's coming!

This is one area I find moms struggle to prioritize the most because they don't always see the value of learning. But since you and I are hanging out here in this book, I know you get it!

Adding in time for you to learn and grow—whether it's a skill, mindset, or professional learning—can do wonders for your confidence and happiness.

I'm not asking you to take three hours a day to read a book or spend your entire weekend finishing an online course. What I'm asking is "Do you think you're worth taking fifteen minutes a day?"

Fifteen minutes a day can be one chapter of a book. Fifteen minutes a day can be one lesson in an online course. Fifteen minutes a day can be a short podcast episode.

Whatever you want to learn, I want you to add it into your planner so you don't miss out. Make sure you're as detailed as possible and write down exactly which chapter, podcast episode, or lesson you'll be doing on what day and during which time block.

I know it can feel daunting to try to add in time for you, but having learning goals for yourself is a form of self-care. One of my clients Cynthia M. has had some major mindset shifts in the past few years working with me on the 15 Minute Formula and her mindset.

Cynthia told me, "Until I met you, I didn't read personal development books at all." And while she was able to sneak in some fiction, she struggled to find time or see the value in picking up anything learning related. She now crushes her reading goals and has so many big a-ha breakthroughs when it comes to her limiting beliefs.

As a busy mom of two little ones, Cynthia had felt stuck in the day to day after leaving work to stay home with them. Between all the learning she did on her own and in the program, she's been able to find more joy in her days, even when they aren't perfect. She works to give herself more grace and the love she knows she deserves. Cynthia and I check in regularly, and she's always updating me on something she's learned about herself and ways she can apply it into her life.

And she did this in just fifteen minutes a day. It wasn't about overwhelming herself with hours and hours of coursework or reading. It was small actions that led to massive mindset changes!

One of my favorite parts of our Sunday planning process in the Club is hearing what the other moms are doing for learning. They often inspire me to try out new hobbies I wouldn't have thought of before (many of them are learning new languages, scrapbooking, or learning to knit) or suggesting great books or podcasts I would never have thought of.

If you're new to this concept of learning for your mindset, I think podcasts are a great way to get started. Every smart phone has an app where you can download these free audios, and you can learn from people from all over the world! My podcast, *The Purpose Driven Mom* podcast is a great place to start, and we have two episodes a week. On Mondays, we share a fifteen-minute or less quick productivity tip (so perfect to add to your learning for the week), and on Thursdays, we air a deep dive interview or teaching from me all around your goals, time management, or productivity.

Whatever it is you choose to do or where you get started, the key here is to schedule it on Sundays so that you can just get going when learning time happens and not have to figure out what you'll be doing next!

time block sample

	MONDAY	TUESDAY	WEDNESDAY	THURSDAY	FRIDAY	SATURDAY	SUNDAY
6:00 am	reading	reading	reading	reading	reading	reading	reading
7:00 am							
8:00 am				Class party			
9:00 am	decluttering	decluttering	decluttering	↓	decluttering		
10:00 am							
11:00 am						Birthday party	
12:00 pm						↓	
1:00 pm						decluttering	
2:00 pm							
3:00 pm					Dentist		
4:00 pm							
5:00 pm		Dance class					
6:00 pm							
7:00 pm	eve. routine	eve. routine	Church	eve. routine	eve. routine	eve. routine	
8:00 pm							
9:00 pm			↓				
10:00 pm			eve. routine				

Step 5: Fill the Rest Up and Pick Your Big 3

Okay, the hard part is done. Now check out your schedule. All I suggested was forty-five minutes each day for you. Forty-five minutes a day for your goals and what lights you up.

I bet if you look at your planner, you'll see you still have a bunch of time left for everything else. When we plan in the traditional sense, we often add in all those little things first and then don't have time for our goals. But by planning with the 15 Minute Formula framework, you make time for you first and still have time to fit the rest in.

Now that your goals are planned, go ahead and add all the little things—the errands, the phone calls, and all the things everyone else needs from you. This method is not saying to ignore everyone else; it's just asking you to focus on you first and for just a short period of time.

(By the way, can we pause here to say you are so worth this time. I know that you might feel guilty about taking any time for yourself and planning your stuff first, but you deserve those forty-five minutes—heck, you deserve more than forty-five minutes.)

One of the ways I like to structure the rest of my schedule, instead of just plopping things in and filling up every line of my planner just because there is a line there (come on, you know you do it too) is to pick my big three or micro priorities for each block.

We talked already about micro priorities for each season, and we've set themes for our time blocks—now let's add them together.

I don't like to put more than three "must do" things in each time block. I know that often life is going to throw me curveballs and I won't get done all I need to get done. Before I plan the day, I like to ask myself to pick out my big three "must do" activities per block. This ensures that my schedule doesn't get too jam packed and that I have a focus for my blocks.

For example, let's go back to the blocks we made in Chapter 5. I've done my best to create my themes and now I've added in time for must-keep appointments, goals, habits, and learning. It's time to determine what my big three are outside of that. Before I do that, my schedule might look light in some place while some blocks will already have one to three things inside of them. Below you can see what was already added and where they fit in the planning process.

6:00 a.m. – 9:00 a.m. self-care and Mommy
Workout (goal)
Morning routine (routine)

9:00 a.m. – 12:00 p.m. home management
Daily cleaning (routine)

12:00 p.m. – 3:00 p.m. Mommy time
Kids' doctor's appointments (appointment)
Audiobook learning (learning)

3:00 p.m. – 7:00 p.m. family time
Swim lessons (appointment)

7:00pm—11:00 p.m. personal and relationship time
Declutter kids' toys (goal)
TV with hubby (goal)

As you can see some blocks are more full than others, but each block has a little space for me to add in a tiny task or something else I want to accomplish. When I plan on Sundays, most days look like this with gaps in the schedule. Then each night before bed, I go into tomorrow's plan and fill in the rest of my tasks and micro priorities based on what happened today or stuff that popped up. I don't suggest planning your whole week out where each block is filled at the start of the week because we know something is going to pop up, get behind, or need to get added. When we start the week with a jam-packed schedule, you're not leaving room for life to happen.

Let's pretend the schedule below is my schedule for Tuesday. On Monday night, I would go in and add in my additional tasks (on top of my goal time) so that all my other to-dos for the day were covered and planned.

6:00 a.m. – 9:00 a.m. self-care and Mommy

Workout (goal)

Morning routine (routine)

Print out papers to drop off at the doctor's

9:00 a.m. – 12:00 p.m. home management

Daily cleaning (routine)

Call Mom

15-minute pick up of downstairs

12:00 p.m. – 3:00 p.m. Mommy time

Kids' doctor's appointments (appointment)

Audiobook (learning)

Run to Target for milk, bread, and birthday gift

3:00 p.m. – 7:00 p.m. family time

Swim lessons (appointment)

Play a family game

Laundry time

7:00pm—11:00 p.m. personal and relationship time

> Declutter kids' toys (goal)
> TV with hubby (goal)
> *Answer text messages and emails*

In doing this nightly, you have a clear plan of your micro priorities and still have time for goals and tiny tasks. If during your blocks you have extra time, awesome! Work on another goal, scroll your phone, or heat up your coffee to enjoy! If you only get those three things done per block, that's great too! Not everything can be equally important, but it's key to make sure you and your goals are at the top of the list!

Priority Brain Dumps Are Your New Best Friend

I know we've established that I love a good list and you probably do too. But have you ever gotten lost in your to-do list? You know you have a million things to get done so you get them out of your brain and onto paper (Go you! Writing things down is a great way to clear out the clutter in your mind!), but as soon as you look down at your paper, the overwhelm begins.

How will you get it all done? Did you really just fill up a page front and back with everything you have to get done? Where will you even start?

One of the routines that I've added into my productivity that has been a game changer is doing a priority brain dump either at the end of a week on Friday to close things out or on Sundays to get focused for the start of the week. Priority brain dumps are like an up-leveled to-do list and leave you ready to take action, not just wanting to throw the list in the trash!

The first step is still to start with your no-filter brain dump. Put on a five-minute timer and write down a major list of what needs to get done to end or start your week (or month or quarter—you can use these whenever). We'll organize all of these tasks next, but I want you to just get it out of your head. While I know looking at it can feel overwhelming, getting it on paper will help clear up your thoughts and allow you to determine top priorities.

Now that you've got your big list, have no fear! It's time to determine what needs to work on and when so that you aren't just left with a huge task list that you ignore because it's overwhelming.

Filtering with the Eisenhower Matrix

When I first got into learning about productivity and getting my own certifications, I attended a productivity workshop presented by the team over at Franklin/Covey, which specializes in helping businesses manage their time and be more productive. One of the tools that they taught was using the Eisenhower matrix to organize your thoughts. I've taken this Eisenhower matrix and tweaked it to fit the 15 Minute Formula to be perfect for moms!

	URGENT	NOT URGENT
IMPORTANT	*do now*	*do later*
NOT IMPORTANT	*delegate*	*drop*

There are four quadrants you are going to put your tasks in. Let's review them first and then incorporate these quadrants with your priority list to get organized.

Quadrant 1: Urgent and Important a.k.a. DO NOW!

Things that belong in quadrant one are tasks that have to be done with urgency. If you're making this list on Sunday for your week, anything in quad one needs to be something that *has* to get done by the end of the week. If it can be done next week, it does *not* belong here!

As a mom, you might find that most of your life is stuck in quadrant one—and that's not a good feeling. Quadrant one tasks often leave us feeling like we're putting out fires, scrambling, and feeling super stressed. I try to get to tasks before they become items that need to go in quadrant one, but inevitably, things pop up that need to go here.

Things you might put in quadrant one might include last-minute phone calls, trips to the store to get that one thing for a project, or paperwork that must be filled out before your kid joins an activity.

Quadrant 2: Non-Urgent and Important a.k.a. DO LATER!

Quadrant two is my favorite and where I like to "live" most days. These are tasks that are important to you but don't need to be done in a rush. I always tend to have a lot of tasks here because this is where I put things I need to plan, things that are due later in my quarterly planning, and tasks that are honestly a bit more fun. This quadrant can also include tasks that need to get done in the next month but aren't in quad one because you have more time to complete them.

You might add in activities such as planning out a birthday party that is in the next few months, working on a fun home decorating project, or completing the school paperwork that isn't due for three weeks.

Quadrant 3: Urgent and Non-Important a.k.a. DELEGATE!

Before we jump into some examples of quad three activities, you'll notice that this quadrant is all about the things that are urgent and need to be done but might be considered non-important. I tend to refer to this quadrant as the delegation quadrant because while things might have to get done right away, they don't have to get done *by you*. They might be non-important to you but important to someone else, and lots of these types of activities often fall into our laps.

Things that you put into this box might have to get done that week or whatever your time frame is for this brain dump, but someone else can do them.

You might add things like bake cupcakes for a bake sale, but your kid is in high school and signed up themselves so they can make them; a cleaning task around that house that needs to get done ASAP, but one of your kiddos can do it (and trust me, they are super capable! If I need the windows or baseboards cleaned before a party or event, my six-year-old can do it!); or a work task that got handed to you that really isn't your jurisdiction.

Quadrant 4: Non-Urgent and Non-Important a.k.a. DROP!

Drop activities are our procrastination tools. While I am not saying everything in quadrant four needs to get dropped forever, you might look at dropping these tasks over the course of the week and picking them up later. Sometimes things you put in quad four this week could potentially become a quad three or quad two later on.

Planning is a great example of this. I've learned that I tend to use planning as a procrastination tool. If I don't feel like actually doing something, I'll plan something else out to distract me. You might do this with organization. You know you need to get the laundry put away, but doesn't that spice rack look like it could use some TLC? It's easy to justify reorganizing it at the moment because it's a "productive" activity, but if it pulls you away from something in your quad one or quad two, it might just be a quad four.

My quadrant four also may have things like catching up on that Netflix show I wanted to watch or hiding away for two hours to read a new novel. While these things are fine, I do believe doing them excessively when you know you're doing them to procrastinate is when you get into trouble.

Now that you understand the quadrants (and grabbed a print out of Quadrant Matrix in your action guide), let's refer back to your big brain dump list that you started with. We're going to create our own quadrants to plop in your tasks and truly prioritize. I suggest making this on lined paper so that you have to limit yourself. Once a box is full—it's full and you can't add anything else to it. And don't feel like you have to fill each box—just use the tasks you wrote down to get organized. Adding more to your task list doesn't mean you're more productive or better; it just means you added more things to your list.

Filter through your list and add in tasks to whichever quadrant they best fit in—and I say "best" because it's not going to be perfect, and some things don't fit the formula. That's okay! Remember intention over perfection always.

As you add something to your quadrant chart, highlight or check it off on your paper. Slowly, you'll start to filter through your tasks and fill up your chart in an order that makes a little bit more sense.

Now, when you're doing your weekly planning (or whenever you use this), you can start with adding in quadrant one activities and making sure they have a place as your big three inside the time blocks. Since those are the most urgent to get done this week, we want to make sure you're planning time for them.

Next, move to your quad two tasks and start to fill them into your planner for the week. By the time you're done with this, you might not have any more spaces inside your time blocks for tasks, and this is okay. Because now that it's time to move to quad three, you have some choices.

If you have space in your blocks (remember, try to pick no more than three micro priorities per block), you can add in a quadrant three activity instead of delegating it or plan out time for some quadrant four fun! It's up to you if you want to help your daughter with those cupcakes or schedule an hour to rewatch an episode of *Buffy the Vampire Slayer*. You also have the option to leave some space blank. You don't have to fill everything in, and if you're following the time-blocking formula from Chapter 5, you'll already have thought catcher time blank. Don't fill that in at all!

Now that you've got your list and planner ready, get moving! Using the priority brain dump has taken that big old to-do list and made it into a focused task list that makes sense for your week!

Chapter 14 Action Steps

1. Start using the weekly planning system this upcoming week. Don't forget a copy of these tasks are in the Action Guide over at www.the15minuteformula.com/free.

2. Do a big brain dump and use the priority matrix to organize all the thoughts and tasks swimming in your head.

PILLAR #5

HABITS

Chapter 15

Creating Habits That Stick

Before we jump into this chapter, I want to pause and applaud you.

Yup. Feel free to stand up, walk around, and take a bow. Because I know that many people who purchase books rarely actually get to the end. Many people might read books and not implement them, and many people know they want to buy a book but never take the leap.

But you, my friend. You're here. You're excited. And you're ready to tackle these goals.

We've covered a ton: from creating your vision and micro priorities to breaking down all your goals and scheduling time to actually work on them.

There is one key thing we haven't dove into yet and that's how we actually make these habits stick.

In Chapter 9, we dove into routine stacking and how to break down your habit-based goals. In this chapter, I want to really give you some practical strategies on how to make new behaviors become things that are long term for you (or how to stop habits you know aren't supporting your goals).

Utilizing Habit Triggers

Every time I start a new habit, I get so excited and ready to go, but by Tuesday something has happened and I've forgotten what habits I was working on and my Monday Mentality kicks back in.

It wasn't until I learned about the concept of habit triggers that things started to stick for good.

When adding a new habit into your day, it's key to anchor it into your current habits and the things that naturally just happen for you. We all have these habits whether we realize them or not.

You get up in the morning and go right to the bathroom to brush your teeth. You walk in the house and hang your bag in the same spot. You go to the bathroom for a break and open your phone to scroll Instagram (maybe just me?).

Habits can take a while to form but luckily for you, you've been forming them your entire life. What we're going to do now is tie your new habit into an older and more established one to help this new one stick for good.

Once you have broken down your habit- or routine-based goal, you'll have a good vision and idea of what you're hoping to accomplish and what it looks like.

Start with breaking your time blocks down and asking yourself, "What habits do I already have during these blocks that I just do naturally?" This is the best way to find habits to easily anchor into.

Your list might look something like this:

6:00 a.m. – 9:00 a.m. self-care and Mommy

- bathroom as soon as I wake up
- check my phone
- brush my teeth
- make my coffee
- load the dishwasher after breakfast

9:00 a.m. – 12:00 p.m. home management

- make lunches
- check the mail
- make another cup of coffee

12:00 p.m. – 3:00 p.m. Mommy time

- story time before nap
- scroll my phone while I rock the baby to sleep

3:00 p.m. – 7:00 p.m. family time

- start dinner

- load dishwasher
- give kids a bath

7:00 p.m. – 11:00 p.m. personal and relationship time

- chat with hubby after kids go to bed
- brush teeth
- wash face
- scroll my phone before bed

As you can see in the above example, I already have habits that I just do because they are second nature, and I bet you have a ton of them as well. Because we do them all the time, we forget about what's already established—whether it's a "good" habit or a "bad" habit.

Once you've gone ahead and determined what your current habits are, it's time to anchor your new ones into them and create habit triggers.

Filtering through your list of goals and habits, predetermine when you want to accomplish the goal and which current habit you have that supports it best.

Before I did this, I was really struggling to hit my reading goals. I had a few audiobooks that I wanted to dive into but kept forgetting to push play. This led me to believe that I "didn't have time" to read or listen to the book.

I decided it was time to create a habit trigger around this since it was important to me and my season. I started to evaluate my current habits and pick what time of day would be best for me to complete the audiobook.

I knew that a consistent habit I had was getting dressed and ready for the day. No matter what, it was something I did and often something I did alone (with my kids running in and out of the room in between playing and fighting). This seemed like the perfect time and habit in which to pair my reading/listening.

I created a proactive plan so that as soon as I got out of the shower (and if you have an iPhone, you can do this in the shower since they are waterproof), I would push play on the audiobook I had already predetermined to read. Since this was a numerical goal, I also knew exactly how many chapters/pages I needed to listen to a day to finish at the end of the month, so I had extra urgency to stay on track.

While I was getting ready (my consistent habit), I was growing a new habit of listening to an audiobook. This had multiple benefits above just completing my reading goal. I prefer to listen to nonfiction over fiction when it comes to audio, so I was increasing my learning and growth time. I was able to work on limiting beliefs and learn new skills. And because I was doing this first thing in the morning, my days tended to start off better because I was putting positive stuff into my brain.

One of my clients , Jamie C. has been using habit triggers for almost a year now, and it's taken things that felt impossible and made them things that she easily can stick with each day. Jamie had been struggling to make an exercise routine stick for years. She knew that working out was good for her but for some reason couldn't make it happen consistently.

She decided to combine using habit triggers with routine stacking and now is able to get her exercise in almost daily! She picked a specific show that she would play for her young kids while she exercised. Most kids' shows are about twenty minutes, which was exactly how much time she needed. By tying the show in with working out, her brain now has a reminder, she has some urgency, and her daily exercise is now just something she does because it's a habit that stuck.

Look back at your time blocks and ask yourself,

- What habits do I already have?
- What time of day do I want to work on my goal?
- Which existing habit makes sense to attach this new habit to?

It's key to make sure you ask yourself the final question: Does this new habit make sense to attach to an existing habit?

For me, listening to the nonfiction book worked because I could process while I got ready. I love learning, so I'm often taking courses to grow personally and professionally. And while listening to a lesson or watching it while I get ready is super similar to listening to an audiobook, I wouldn't attach my learning to getting ready.

Why not?

Well, here is the thing: if I am learning or taking a course and trying to deeply process the information, I can't do that while I get ready because I might want to stop and take notes. Stopping to take notes would prolong getting ready, and that habit would more likely get me frustrated about the goal and want to quit.

Instead, I could attach this new habit to something else during my day or replace a nonpreferable habit with this new one.

As you saw in my previous example, I wrote down multiple times a day that some established habits are scrolling my phone. I don't think there is anything wrong with scrolling your phone or having down time, but when you find yourself saying you don't have time for your goals, you might want to analyze and see where you can create time and get rid of some habits you know aren't serving you.

Going back to fitting in my learning time, I realized that watching lessons while I got ready wasn't going to work for me. What if I replaced one of my mindless phone scrolling times with a fifteen-minute lesson or module? I found that after the kids went to bed, I was turning to my phone to decompress, which is fine. But what was happening was that fifteen minutes was turning into forty-five minutes and then I didn't want to do anything else except turn into a couch potato.

I decided that I would adjust my nighttime phone scrolling habit so that before I went to scroll my phone, I would spend just fifteen minutes learning. I wasn't completely giving up my relaxation time, but since I knew I was already spending thirty to forty-five minutes on the phone, I could use even half that time to learn and still get in a good scroll.

Using the 15 Minute Formula isn't about going a million miles an hour and striving toward being the most productive person 100% of the time. It's about creating adjustments in the way you do your schedule to allow you to live your life (or scroll your phone) *and* go after your goals.

I found after just a few days of this that I was finally making progress on the course I was taking without feeling "Goodness, when do I get to relax?" I knew that my relaxing scroll time was coming after I watched that lesson and took my notes. After a few weeks, many of those fifteen-minute sessions turned into thirty-minute sessions, and I completed the course faster than I planned!

How to Ditch a Bad Habit

We've talked a lot about creating habits and achieving your goals so far, but what if you have a habit you want to get rid of?

I don't like to classify habits into good and bad, but since they're common terms we've always used, I'll use it interchangeably with the word "unfavorable."

An unfavorable or bad habit is one that just doesn't suit you for this season of life. Now there are habits that are bad for your health and super toxic, and I know we're familiar with those, but we sometimes also start to create unfavorable habits that just don't support our goals for the current season.

You may have gotten into a habit of complaining about a coworker every time you have lunch with someone at work. Or maybe you find you're watching TV more than you'd like as an escape and would just like to decrease the amount of TV you watch. Watching TV isn't a bad thing, but it's unfavorable since the excessive amounts of TV might be taking you away from your goals.

We know habits are created over time, and it can take some work to change them, but it's totally possible. There are a few simple steps you can use to get there.

Step 1: Gather Your Data

I'm sure you've guessed at this point that I'm a data lover. I think that we often jump into things emotionally (and by "we," I am pointing the finger at me too), and before we start shaming ourselves for being terrible and the reason we never achieve things, let's take a step back and figure out *why*.

When I'm trying to ditch a habit, I like to take a few days to figure out more about it. Let's put on our detective hats and do some research!

Split your paper in three so we can track some key things (and you can grab a worksheet to do this at www. the15minuteformula.com/free in the action guide).

Label the left column Antecedent, the middle Habit, and the right Result.

We're going to take some time to figure out a few things before making our plan. Over the course of one to three days, every time your unfavorable habit occurs, you're going to jot these things down.

The first thing to jot down is the habit. Whenever the actual bad habit occurs, write down what exactly it was and what it looked like. This could be biting your nails, scrolling your phone, complaining, or binge eating. Throughout the day, add to your Habit column anytime that specific habit or a similar one occurs. This could simply be "grabbed snack" or "went through drive through" if you're unfavorable habit is stress eating.

After you've got the habit jotted down, I suggest you fill in the Antecedent. An antecedent is something that happens right before a behavior occurs. When I was a special education teacher, I would create Positive Behavioral Support Plans, and one of the most important pieces of information needed to complete this was figuring out what happened right before the behavior.

It's important to realize your antecedent because then you can make a plan to change the things that are triggering you (which we'll look at in Step 2).

You might write down that right after you get off the phone with your mom, you notice you start biting your nails. Or as soon as you get home from work, you head right to the snack cabinet. Perhaps you notice that you always yell at the kids in the morning right before going to school.

The final thing you'll want to chart is the result of completing that habit. This could be either a positive or negative consequence or reinforcement that this behavior gives you. Running to the snack cabinet might result in you ignoring the stress of the day for a minute. Yelling at your kids might result in you feeling like a bad mom. And biting your nails gives you a release for the anxiety you got from the phone call with your mom.

Step 2: Realize Your Triggers

Once you've done this for a few days, you should have a decent amount of data to figure out why your habit is happening.

Do an analysis of the behaviors in order to note the frequency or how many times a day this behavior occurs. If you know how many times you're doing something, we can use the habit scaffolding method to lessen it to a place you feel better about.

You should also pay a lot of attention to common antecedents. Are you always complaining about the same coworker? Does the splashing that your kids do in the bath drive you over the edge and cause you to yell? Do you have the same negative voice telling you that you can't achieve a goal after you do a certain task?

Realizing these patterns does a few things. First, it helps you see and recognize that there are reasons your habit exists and it's not just because you're bad or awful (or whatever that negative voice continues to tell you). Second, it can show you what patterns stand out the most for you so you can make a great plan around ditching this unfavorable habit.

Step 3: Create a Plan

Now that you know your patterns, it's time to make a plan that makes sense for you. I'll see people who want to quit smoking and they hear that nicotine gums helped a friend so it *has* to work for them. They try the same gum and hope for the best. Quickly, they notice things don't seem to be working as easily as they hoped.

It's because they tried to make a plan to eliminate a habit that wasn't customized for them. And customizing is exactly what you'll need to do with all your data.

Say after figuring the triggers out (to the best of my ability), I realize that I'm picking up my phone to scroll social media for two hours a day.

I don't think there is anything wrong with scrolling my phone that much, but I realize this behavior is excessive for me. Instead of going cold turkey and saying I'll never go on my phone again, I decide to use habit scaffolding to get to where I want to be.

With habit scaffolding, I am going to take my time on social media and slowly decrease it to get to my end result. Remember, it's not about doing it all at once and setting myself up to quit, it's about small changes that will create those lifelong results and habits.

My plan could look like this:

Week 0 (baseline) = 2 hours a day scrolling Facebook

Week 1 Goal = 1 hour and 45 minutes a day

Week 2 Goal = 1 hour and 30 minutes a day

Week 3 Goal = 1 hour and 15 minutes a day

Week 4 Goal = 1 hour a day

Now I've got a plan that has freed me up an hour a day and still get an hour to laugh at *Grumpy Cat* memes while I wait in the car line. Win-win.

Pro tip: If you do have a phone related goal, see if your phone tracks how much time you spend on your phone and specifically how much time you spend per app. If my goal was to decrease my Facebook time, I could set limits on Facebook to turn off the app after 1 hour and 45 minutes. By using this built-in phone feature, you don't need to time yourself or try to keep track each time you open up for a two-minute scroll. Your phone will do the hard work for you, and when your time is up, it's done!

If it's too much of a distraction, you can also take the app completely off your phone. I started to take Facebook off my phone once I hit my limit and for the whole day on Saturday.

If when analyzing your triggers, you notice that you have some antecedent patterns, you might want to make some additional goals to help you decrease the specific habit. I'll be honest, these ones are harder to track and determine and often require hard work to get rid of but are totally worth it.

What if in my analysis I realized that every time I came home from work, I was super stressed and reached for the snack cabinet? I know that the stress at work is what is causing me to emotionally eat, and I want to change it.

There are a few ways you can attack the antecedent to work to change the behavior. I could start with changing the snacks I keep in the house. If something I deem unhealthy isn't in the house, I am less likely to grab at it. Now, while I think this is a good strategy, I think it's also a Band-Aid to the real problem.

Because the real problem here is the amount of stress I am taking home after work. I am sure that there are other consequences that stress is having in my life and snacking is just one of them.

What if instead of just trying to limit the snacking, I came up with some proactive strategies to help the stress. My list might look like this:

- Create a playlist of calming music to listen to on the ride home.
- Put affirmation Post-its on my dashboard to remind me that I deserve to be calm and present at home.
- Tell my family that I am working on my boundaries and give them things they can do to help me when they notice I am bringing that stress home
- Read a book on self-compassion and confidence to empower me to create better boundaries at work.
- Make sure to leave work at a certain time and say no when last-minute things come up.

While these things aren't as easy to implement and take a lot more inner work, by identifying and recognizing these as triggers, you can become empowered to fix them and feel more aligned—instead of just throwing your hands in the air and saying "it is what it is."

Chapter 15 Action Steps

1. Make your list of habit triggers and a plan for your goals around them.
2. Complete an Antecedent–Habit–Result chart for an unfavorable behavior you want to change. And don't forget to download the action plan where we've got a workbook full of these charts ready for you.

Chapter 16

Keeping Your Momentum Going

I know what it's like to have the best intentions in the world, get so excited, put all the work in on your goal, and then get tossed off course. It can be so hard when you get off track on vacation, because of a life event, or just when normal day-to-day stressors derail your goal plan.

If you begin to implement the 15 Minute Formula and these sorts of things happen, I want to encourage you to keep going.

Keep showing up for your goals when they seem hard. Keep showing up for your goals when you aren't making progress. And keep showing up for you.

You deserve it.

You deserve all the work you put into your plan. You deserve the time pockets you're going to sneak in to improve and better yourself. You deserve to do something just for you.

But let's talk some truth right now. Because you're going to get started. You're going to close this book and be so jazzed and ready to go. And then things will pause or even stop.

A kid needs you. A work project takes over. You feel the guilt of the mounds of laundry staring at you and the dishes you know need to put away.

And you'll start to talk yourself out of working on your goals. You'll tell yourself that you can start that business when your kids go back to school. You'll convince yourself that other moms are stressed out too, so this is just what motherhood is supposed to feel like. You'll remind yourself of your failures and convince yourself nothing will ever stick when it comes to your goals and time management.

Then you'll see other people doing what you want to do. That girl training for that half marathon could be you, but you have young kids. That mom starting her business might be you, but you don't have the support from your partner. Those moms posting about their evening routines who look like their houses are in order must have more help or be better at managing their time.

But not you. You'll never be like them.

Well, that part is actually true.

You will never be like them.

And you're not meant to be.

You were created to be you—with all your amazing flaws and obstacles that stand in your way. You are you with all your past experiences that have made you the person you are today. And you are you even after repeated failures that make you feel unworthy.

But you're not unworthy.

You're incredible.

You're going to fail. Probably a lot.

And that's okay.

Starting to wrap your brain around the fact that things won't look perfectly and that your life will never be the same as someone else's is the first step to creating your more aligned life.

The goal of the 15 Minute Formula and the priority-based productivity models we covered in this book are to help you create routines and plans for your time around *your* life.

Not your neighbors, not that Instagram influencer, and not what your mother-in-law tells you it needs to be.

I hope we've hung out long enough that you have given yourself permission to embrace creating a plan for you.

And if not, permission granted.

It's okay to say no to things that don't make sense for your family right now. It's okay to say yes to things that may feel frivolous but bring you joy. It's more than okay to take time for things that matter to you and not just fill up every line of your planner based on what others make you feel you must do.

It's time to stop "should-ing" yourself.

When you catch yourself in statements like "I should be doing" or "I shouldn't make time for,"

STOP.

When you "should" on yourself, you are taking a limiting belief that has been implanted in your heart and brain and making it a reality.

Ask yourself where these "should" statements are coming from and work to remove them from your vocabulary.

Because the only thing you "should" be doing is what aligns for you—not society, not friends from high school, and not coworkers. You, your family, your goals, and your priorities.

You deserve it. You're worth it. And you're capable of achieving it.

You've got this!

Chapter 16 Action Steps

1. Let's touch base! Email book@apurposedrivenmom. com or send me a direct message on Instagram (@ apurposedrivenmom) and let me know you read the book so I can celebrate you!

Endnotes

1 Jon Gordon, Jimmy Page, and Dan Britton, *One Word That Will Change Your Life* (New Jersey: Wiley Publishing, 2013).

2 Darren Hardy, *Compound Effect* (New York: Vanguard Press, 2012).

3 Mark Murphy, "This Is the Month When New Year's Resolutions Fail—Here's How to Save Them," *Forbes*, accessed November 12, 2021, https://www.forbes.com/sites/markmurphy/2020/02/11/this-is-the-month-when-new-years-resolutions-fail-heres-how-to-save-them/?sh=50130f23272f.

Thanks so much for reading!

I am so thankful for you and the time you spent hanging out with me in this book!

Can I ask you favor?

If this book encouraged you in anyway, please scan the QR code below and head over to leave it a review! Reviews mean a lot and they help other people find this book and our community!

www.ingramcontent.com/pod-product-compliance
Lightning Source LLC
Chambersburg PA
CBHW071151130626
46553CB00004B/1615